AF797936

Investment Strategies In A Crazy Economy

Book Summary:

Investing can seem daunting, but at its core, it's about putting your money to work so it can grow over time. Think of it like planting a seed: you put in a little effort (your money), and with time and care (smart investment choices), it can blossom into something much larger. There are many ways to invest, each with different levels of risk and potential reward. One common approach is to invest in stocks, which represent ownership in a company. If the company does well, the value of your stock may increase, and you could make money by selling it. However, if the company struggles, the value of your stock could decrease, and you could lose money.

Another option is bonds, which are essentially loans you make to a government or company. They generally offer lower returns than stocks but are considered less risky. A key strategy for most non- investors is diversification – don't put all your eggs in one basket! Spread your investments across different types of assets (like stocks and bonds) and different companies or sectors. This helps to reduce the overall risk if one investment performs poorly. Another important concept is long-term investing. Investing is a marathon, not a sprint. It's better to focus on steady growth over the long term, rather than trying to make quick profits, which often leads to higher risk.

Finally, before investing any money, it's essential to understand your own risk tolerance and financial goals. Consider how much risk you're comfortable with and how much time you have before you need the money. Resources like books, websites, and financial advisors can help you learn more and make informed decisions. Remember, starting small and learning as you go is perfectly acceptable.

Dedication:

This book is dedicated to all those who strive for financial security in the face of economic uncertainty. It is a testament to the resilience of the human spirit and the power of knowledge to navigate turbulent times. To those who have faced setbacks and learned from their experiences, to those who are tirelessly working towards their financial goals, and to those who are bravely venturing into the complexities of the investment world, this book is for you.

May it serve as a beacon of hope, providing the tools and insights necessary to build a brighter and more secure financial future. It is a guide born from a deep understanding of the challenges faced by everyday investors, a culmination of years of experience and a commitment to fostering financial literacy and empowerment. This is not just a manual of investment strategies; it is a companion on your journey to financial freedom, offering encouragement and practical advice to help you achieve your dreams and secure a comfortable retirement, no matter how volatile the economy may become. My hope is that this book empowers you to confidently manage your finances, fostering not just wealth, but peace of mind.

Preface:

Navigating the financial landscape today is akin to sailing uncharted waters. Economic volatility, unpredictable market swings, and a constant barrage of information can leave even seasoned investors feeling disoriented. This book isn't intended to offer foolproof solutions or guarantees of riches. Instead, it aims to equip you, the reader, with the knowledge and understanding necessary to make informed decisions in these uncertain times. My experience as a financial advisor has shown me that success in investing isn't about predicting the future but about understanding your own financial goals, risk tolerance, and the fundamentals of sound investment strategies.

This book provides a framework for achieving that understanding.

Through clear explanations, practical examples, and a focus on actionable strategies, we will explore diverse investment options, from the familiar to the emerging, enabling you to build a diversified portfolio capable of weathering economic storms. We'll delve into the importance of identifying underperforming assets, mastering fundamental and technical analysis, and leveraging the power of diversification to mitigate risk.

Ultimately, the goal is to empower you to take control of your financial future, fostering confidence and security in your investment decisions. This is your roadmap to building a robust financial plan and navigating the crazy economy with increased confidence and success.

Table Of Content

Introduction:

The economic climate is constantly changing, presenting both opportunities and challenges for investors. For those nearing retirement or already retired, the stakes are especially high.

Securing your financial future in a volatile market requires careful planning and a solid understanding of investment strategies. This book, "Investment Strategies in a Crazy Economy," provides a practical guide for individuals seeking to achieve long-term financial success, regardless of economic conditions.

Whether you are a novice investor or have some experience, this book offers actionable strategies to help you navigate the complexities of today's financial world. We will demystify the jargon often associated with investing, focusing on clear explanations and relatable examples. You'll learn to assess your current financial situation, define your financial goals, and identify your risk tolerance. We'll explore a range of investment vehicles, including traditional options like CDs and annuities, as well as higher-yield accounts and various stock classifications (aggressive, medium- aggressive, and safe low-risk).

We will delve into the world of stocks, examining both fundamental and technical analysis to identify promising stocks with high growth potential and learn how to effectively mitigate risks.

Furthermore, we'll investigate alternative assets such as precious metals and real estate, allowing you to diversify your portfolio and reduce overall risk. Finally, we'll cover retirement planning strategies, including different retirement account options, maximizing savings, and planning for retirement income. This book is your comprehensive guide to building a robust and diversified investment portfolio, enabling you to secure your financial future and achieve long-term financial success. Let's begin this journey together.

Chapter 1: Understanding Your Financial Landscape

Before embarking on any investment strategy, especially in today's volatile economic climate, a thorough understanding of your current financial situation is paramount. This isn't just about knowing how much money you have; it's about gaining a holistic view of your financial health – your strengths, weaknesses, and potential vulnerabilities. This self-assessment forms the bedrock upon which you will build a robust and resilient investment portfolio. Think of it as a financial checkup, crucial for diagnosing potential problems and charting a course toward your financial goals.

The first step is calculating your net worth. This seemingly simple calculation – assets minus liabilities – provides a snapshot of your overall financial position. Assets encompass everything you own of value: cash, savings accounts, checking accounts, investments (stocks, bonds, mutual funds, real estate, retirement accounts like 401(k)s and IRAs), vehicles, and any other property. Liabilities represent your debts: mortgages, student loans, credit card balances, personal loans, and any other outstanding obligations.

The difference between your total assets and total liabilities is your net worth. A positive net worth indicates you own more than you owe, while a negative net worth signals you owe more than you own.

Let's illustrate with examples. Consider a 55-year-old nearing retirement, Jane Doe. Jane has a 401(k) worth $250,000, a savings account with $20,000, a house valued at $300,000 (with a mortgage of $100,000), and a car worth $10,000. Her assets total

$580,000. Her liabilities include the $100,000 mortgage and $5,000 in credit card debt, totaling $105,000. Jane's net worth is $580,000-

$105,000 = $475,000. This represents a healthy financial position, providing a strong foundation for her retirement planning.

Now, let's look at a different scenario. John Smith, a 30-year-old with significant student loan debt, possesses a smaller net worth. He has a savings account with $5,000, a car worth $8,000, and no other assets. However, he has $50,000 in student loan debt and $3,000 in credit card debt, totaling $53,000 in liabilities. John's net worth is

$13,000 - $53,000 = -$40,000. While a negative net worth isn't necessarily catastrophic, it highlights the need for aggressive debt reduction and saving strategies. John needs a more strategic approach to managing his finances.

Calculating net worth is just the starting point. A truly comprehensive assessment requires a detailed analysis of your income and expenses. This involves tracking all sources of income (salary, investments, rental income, etc.) and meticulously documenting your expenses across various categories (housing, food, transportation, entertainment, debt payments, etc.). Numerous budgeting tools and apps can simplify this process, automating the tracking and providing valuable insights into your spending habits.

Many financial institutions offer budgeting tools integrated directly into their online banking platforms. Alternatively, spreadsheets, or even simple notebooks, can be used to manually track income and expenditures.

The key to effective budgeting lies in identifying areas where expenses can be reduced without significantly impacting your lifestyle. This may involve cutting back on non-essential spending, negotiating lower bills with service providers, or finding more affordable alternatives. For instance, reducing daily coffee shop expenses or finding cheaper transportation options can accumulate to significant savings over time. The goal is to create a budget that reflects your financial goals and leaves room for both essential expenses and investment contributions.

Identifying and analyzing your debts is also crucial. Pay close attention to interest rates, payment amounts, and outstanding balances. High-interest debts, such as credit card debt, should be prioritized for repayment as the accumulating interest can significantly impede financial progress. Strategies for debt reduction can range from the debt snowball method (paying off the smallest debt first for psychological encouragement) to the

In contrast, if you're saving for your child's college education ten years from now, you could incorporate a greater allocation to higher- growth investments, accepting a higher degree of risk in the pursuit of potentially higher returns.

The specificity of your goals is critical. Instead of a vague aspiration like "travel more," consider a concrete goal such as "take a three- week European trip in five years, costing $10,000." This level of detail allows you to calculate the amount you need to save each month to achieve your goal and to choose investments appropriate to the timeframe. Similarly, instead of "pay off my mortgage," aim for a more specific goal like "pay off my mortgage of $200,000 within 10 years." This precision allows for a tailored repayment strategy and provides a clear benchmark for your progress.

Once you have clearly defined your financial goals, the next critical step is to determine your risk tolerance. This refers to your comfort level with the potential for loss in your investments. Risk tolerance is subjective, influenced by a variety of factors including your personality, financial situation, time horizon, and overall Investment experience. Some individuals are inherently more risk- averse, prioritizing capital preservation over the potential for high returns. Others possess a higher risk tolerance, willing to accept greater volatility in exchange for potentially higher gains.

Consider two hypothetical investors, both aiming for retirement in 20 years:

Investor A, a 45-year-old with a conservative personality and a secure job, has a low risk tolerance. They prioritize the security of their principal and are more comfortable with lower but predictable returns. Their investment portfolio might consist primarily of low-risk options like government bonds, high-yield savings accounts, and dividend-paying stocks of established companies. They are less likely to allocate substantial capital to higher-risk investments like individual stocks of small-cap companies or speculative ventures in emerging markets. Their focus is on preserving capital and generating steady, if modest, returns.

Investor B, a 30-year-old with a higher risk tolerance and a long- term time horizon, can afford to take on more risk. They are more comfortable with market fluctuations and the potential for short- term losses in pursuit of potentially higher long-term gains. Their Portfolio might include a larger allocation to equities, including growth stocks and emerging market investments. They may also consider alternative investments, such as real estate or private equity, although these often come with reduced liquidity. Their focus is on capital appreciation over the long term, accepting the possibility of higher volatility along the way.

It's important to recognize that risk tolerance isn't static. It can shift over time based on changes in your financial circumstances, life events, or your overall outlook. A sudden job loss, for instance, might cause you to become more risk-averse, leading you to reassess your investment strategy and shift towards lower-risk options.

Conversely, receiving a significant inheritance could increase your risk tolerance and allow you to consider more aggressive investment strategies.

Determining your risk tolerance is not just about your personality; it's also about your financial situation. Individuals with a larger financial cushion and a lower debt burden generally have a greater capacity to absorb losses and hence, can tolerate higher levels of risk. Those with limited financial resources or significant debts should prioritize capital preservation and adopt a more conservative investment approach.

The concept of a time horizon is also crucial. Younger investors with longer time horizons can usually afford to take on more risk as they have more time to recover from potential short-term losses. As you approach retirement, your time horizon shrinks, and your risk tolerance naturally decreases. Your investment strategy should reflect this changing dynamic.

There are several methods for assessing your risk tolerance. Many online questionnaires and financial planning tools can help you gauge your risk profile. However, it's also crucial to reflect on your own comfort level with potential losses, your financial circumstances, and your long-term goals. Remember, there's no one-size-fits-all approach. The right level of risk is highly individual, dependent upon your specific circumstances and aspirations. Ultimately, the goal is to find a balance between risk and reward

That aligns with your financial goals and risk tolerance. This doesn't mean avoiding risk altogether; some level of risk is often necessary to achieve significant long-term growth. Instead, it's about identifying an appropriate level of risk that you are comfortable with and that allows you to achieve your objectives without jeopardizing your financial security. This may require diversifying your portfolio across different asset classes, spreading your investments across various sectors and geographies to mitigate the impact of potential losses.

Regularly reviewing your financial goals and risk tolerance is crucial as your life circumstances evolve. Periodically revisiting these assessments ensures that your investment strategy remains

Aligned with your current situation, allowing you to adapt to changing conditions and make informed decisions that will continue to propel you toward your financial aspirations. Remember, effective financial planning is an ongoing process, requiring continuous monitoring and adjustment to optimize your results. The proactive management of your financial goals and risk tolerance is a cornerstone of successful long-term investment.

Identifying Underperforming Assets in Your Portfolio

Now that we've established your financial goals and assessed your risk tolerance, let's turn our attention to a critical aspect of portfolio management: identifying underperforming assets. This isn't about panic selling; it's about proactive management to optimize your returns and mitigate potential losses. Ignoring underperforming assets can significantly hinder your progress toward your financial goals.

The first step in identifying underperforming assets involves a thorough review of your portfolio's historical performance. This goes beyond simply looking at the overall return; it requires a granular examination of the performance of individual assets. You should analyze the performance of each investment relative to its benchmark, its peers, and its historical performance. For example, if you own shares of a particular company, compare its performance against the broader market index (like the S&P 500) and similar companies in its industry. Consistent underperformance relative to these benchmarks is a red flag.

Don't rely solely on short-term fluctuations. A temporary dip in value doesn't necessarily signal an underperforming asset. However, consistent underperformance over an extended period, say, two or three years, warrants closer scrutiny. Use readily available tools, such as online brokerage platforms and financial analysis websites, to access historical performance data. Many platforms offer charting tools and comparative analysis features that can simplify this process. For example, comparing the performance of a technology stock to the NASDAQ Composite Index or a real estate investment trust (REIT) against a REIT index will provide valuable context.

Understanding market trends and industry factors is equally crucial. Macroeconomic conditions, such as interest rate hikes, inflation, or geopolitical instability, can significantly impact the performance of specific sectors. For instance, rising interest rates generally negatively affect bond prices, while high inflation often erodes the purchasing power of fixed-income investments. Similarly, industry- specific challenges, questionnaires and financial planning tools can help you gauge your risk profile. However, it's also crucial to reflect on your own comfort level with potential losses, your financial circumstances, and your long-term goals. Remember, there's no one-size-fits-all approach. The right level of risk is highly individual, dependent upon your specific circumstances and aspirations. Ultimately, the goal is to find a balance between risk and reward

That aligns with your financial goals and risk tolerance. This doesn't mean avoiding risk altogether; some level of risk is often necessary to achieve significant long-term growth. Instead, it's about identifying an appropriate level of risk that you are comfortable with and that allows you to achieve your objectives without jeopardizing your financial security. This may require diversifying your portfolio across different asset classes, spreading your investments across various sectors and geographies to mitigate the impact of potential losses.

Regularly reviewing your financial goals and risk tolerance is crucial as your life circumstances evolve. Periodically revisiting these assessments ensures that your investment strategy remains

Aligned with your current situation, allowing you to adapt to changing conditions and make informed decisions that will continue to propel you toward your financial aspirations. Remember, effective financial planning is an ongoing process, requiring continuous monitoring and adjustment to optimize your results. The proactive management of your financial goals and risk tolerance is a cornerstone of successful long-term investment.

Identifying Underperforming Assets in Your Portfolio

Now that we've established your financial goals and assessed your risk tolerance, let's turn our attention to a critical aspect of portfolio management: identifying underperforming assets. This isn't about panic selling; it's about proactive management to optimize your returns and mitigate potential losses. Ignoring underperforming assets can significantly hinder your progress toward your financial goals.

The first step in identifying underperforming assets involves a thorough review of your portfolio's historical performance. This goes beyond simply looking at the overall return; it requires a granular examination of the performance of individual assets. You should analyze the performance of each investment relative to its benchmark, its peers, and its historical performance. For example, if you own shares of a particular company, compare its performance against the broader market index (like the S&P 500) and similar companies in its industry. Consistent underperformance relative to these benchmarks is a red flag.

Don't rely solely on short-term fluctuations. A temporary dip in value doesn't necessarily signal an underperforming asset. However, consistent underperformance over an extended period, say, two or three years, warrants closer scrutiny. Use readily available tools, such as online brokerage platforms and financial analysis websites, to access historical performance data. Many platforms offer charting tools and comparative analysis features that can simplify this process. For example, comparing the performance of a technology stock to the NASDAQ Composite Index or a real estate investment trust (REIT) against a REIT index will provide valuable context.

Understanding market trends and industry factors is equally crucial. Macroeconomic conditions, such as interest rate hikes, inflation, or geopolitical instability, can significantly impact the performance of specific sectors. For instance, rising interest rates generally negatively affect bond prices, while high inflation often erodes the purchasing power of fixed-income investments. Similarly, industry- specific challenges, such as increased competition, regulatory changes, or technological disruptions, can significantly impact the performance of individual companies.

Consider the case of a company heavily reliant on fossil fuels. The transition toward renewable energy sources has created headwinds for such companies, impacting their stock prices. Similarly, companies in the retail sector have faced significant challenges due to the rise of e-commerce. Understanding these broader trends allows you to identify assets that are likely to continue underperforming due to unfavorable market dynamics. Staying informed about economic indicators, industry news, and technological advancements is vital in this aspect.

Assessing the potential for future growth is another key element in identifying underperforming assets. This involves analyzing the company's financial statements, assessing its competitive landscape, and considering its growth prospects. Look for signs of declining revenue, shrinking profit margins, increasing debt, or a lack of innovation. These factors can all signal future underperformance.

For instance, a company consistently losing market share to competitors might be a candidate for divestment, despite a seemingly stable present performance. Thorough due diligence is essential here, utilizing resources like company annual reports, financial news articles, and analyst reports.

Let's examine real-world examples of underperforming assets and how to recognize the warning signs. Imagine a company that, despite years of expansion, continually fails to meet its earnings expectations. This might be reflected in consistently missed revenue targets, a declining stock price, and negative analyst sentiment.

Another example could be a bond issued by a company struggling with high debt levels and a weakening credit rating. This increased risk profile will typically manifest as a lower bond price and a reduced yield compared to similar bonds.

Identifying these trends requires diligence and careful analysis. However, simply recognizing underperformance isn't enough. You need strategies for mitigating losses. In some cases, this might involve selling the underperforming asset to limit further losses and reinvest the proceeds into more promising opportunities. However, consider tax implications before making any hasty decisions. Selling an asset at a loss can potentially offset capital gains taxes on other investments, creating a tax advantage. Consult with a tax professional to assess the optimal strategy.

In other situations, you might choose to hold onto the underperforming asset, hoping for a turnaround. This is a riskier approach, but it can be justified if you believe the underlying fundamentals of the company or investment are sound and the current underperformance is temporary. However, this strategy requires careful monitoring and a clear exit strategy – a predetermined point at which you'll sell regardless of the asset's performance.

Regular portfolio reviews are essential to identify underperforming assets. Aim for at least an annual review, but more frequent reviews, perhaps quarterly or even monthly, can be beneficial, especially during periods of market volatility. These reviews shouldn't just focus on historical performance; they should also incorporate current market conditions and your updated financial goals and risk tolerance. A change in your personal circumstances, such as a job loss or a change in your investment horizon, might necessitate shifts in your portfolio allocations.

During these reviews, you should also consider diversification. If a significant portion of your portfolio is concentrated in a particular sector or asset class that is underperforming, you may want to rebalance your portfolio by selling some of those assets and investing in other sectors or asset classes that appear more promising. Diversification is a cornerstone of risk management, helping to mitigate the impact of individual asset underperformance.

Furthermore, consider seeking professional advice. A financial advisor can provide valuable insights based on your specific circumstances and offer tailored strategies for managing underperforming assets. They can help you identify potential blind spots in your analysis and develop an effective action plan. While this involves a cost, the expertise they offer can often be invaluable in guiding long-term investment success and ensuring your portfolio aligns with your evolving needs.

Remember, identifying and addressing underperforming assets is an ongoing process. It requires vigilance, analysis, and a willingness to adapt your investment strategy as circumstances change. By consistently monitoring your portfolio, understanding market trends, and making informed decisions, you can significantly improve your chances of achieving your financial goals. Proactive portfolio management is not merely about reacting to losses; it's about cultivating a robust, dynamic investment strategy that continuously evolves to meet the challenges of a constantly changing economic landscape.

Understanding Different Investment Vehicles

Now that we've laid the groundwork for identifying and managing underperforming assets within your portfolio, let's delve into the diverse world of investment vehicles. Understanding the characteristics and nuances of different investment options is paramount to building a robust and diversified portfolio tailored to your risk tolerance and financial goals. This section will provide a comprehensive overview of various investment vehicles, their associated risks and rewards, and their suitability for different investor profiles.

We'll begin with stocks, the cornerstone of many investment portfolios. Stocks represent ownership shares in a publicly traded company. When you buy a stock, you become a part-owner of that company, and your returns are directly tied to the company's performance. The potential for high returns is a significant advantage of stock investments, but this comes with considerable risk. Stock prices can fluctuate wildly based on a multitude of factors, including company performance, industry trends, economic conditions, and overall market sentiment.

There's a broad spectrum of stocks, catering to varying risk appetites. Aggressive growth stocks, often associated with newer, rapidly expanding companies, offer the potential for substantial returns but carry significantly higher risk. These companies typically reinvest their profits back into the business, prioritizing growth over immediate dividends. Examples include companies in emerging technological fields such as artificial intelligence, biotechnology, or renewable energy. Investing in such companies requires a higher risk tolerance and a longer-term investment horizon, as their stock prices can be significantly more volatile.

Conversely, safe, low-risk stocks typically belong to established, large-cap companies with a history of consistent profitability and dividend payments. These companies tend to be more stable and less susceptible to dramatic price fluctuations, making them suitable for investors seeking capital preservation and steady income. Utility companies and blue-chip companies often fall into this category. Medium-aggressive stocks occupy a middle ground, offering a balance between growth potential and risk mitigation.

Next, we have bonds, which represent debt instruments issued by governments or corporations. When you buy a bond, you're essentially lending money to the issuer for a specified period, receiving regular interest payments (coupons) in return. At the maturity date, you receive the principal amount back. Bonds generally offer lower returns compared to stocks, but they are also considered less risky. Government bonds are typically considered the safest type of bond due to the lower default risk associated with governments. Corporate bonds, on the other hand, carry more risk as the issuer's financial stability can directly influence the bond's value. The interest rate on a bond (its yield) reflects its risk profile.

Higher-risk bonds generally offer higher yields to compensate investors for the increased chance of default. Understanding the credit rating of a bond, which reflects the issuer's creditworthiness, is crucial for evaluating the risk.

Mutual funds provide a diversified approach to investing, pooling money from multiple investors to invest in a portfolio of stocks, bonds, or other assets. This diversification helps mitigate risk by spreading investments across various assets, reducing reliance on the performance of any single security. Mutual funds offer professional management, with fund managers making investment decisions on behalf of investors. However, this comes with management fees, which can eat into returns. Different mutual funds cater to different investment goals and risk profiles, from conservative, low-risk funds focused on capital preservation to aggressive growth funds aiming for high returns. Index funds, a type of mutual fund that mirrors a specific market index (such as the S&P 500), offer broad market exposure at a low cost.

Exchange-traded funds (ETFs) are similar to mutual funds, but they trade on stock exchanges like individual stocks. This means they can be bought and sold throughout the trading day, offering greater flexibility compared to mutual funds, which are typically priced only once at the end of the trading day. ETFs also generally have lower expense ratios than mutual funds. Like mutual funds, ETFs come in various types, mirroring different market sectors or investment strategies. Beyond stocks, bonds, and mutual funds, alternative assets offer diversification and potential higher returns. Gold, for instance, is often seen as a safe haven asset, its value often rising during times of economic uncertainty. However, gold doesn't generate income and its price can be volatile. Real estate, including residential and commercial properties, can offer both income (through rental payments) and appreciation in value over time. However, real estate investing requires significant capital outlay and comes with ongoing expenses, such as property taxes and maintenance. Other alternative investments might include commodities (oil, natural gas, etc.), private equity, and hedge funds, but these often have higher barriers to entry and require significant expertise.

Choosing the right investment vehicle depends on your individual financial goals, risk tolerance, and investment horizon. A younger investor with a longer time horizon might be more comfortable with higher-risk investments like aggressive growth stocks, aiming for significant returns over the long term. An investor closer to retirement, on the other hand, might prioritize capital preservation and opt for lower-risk investments like bonds or conservative mutual funds. This is where a balanced, diversified portfolio plays a vital role. Diversification means spreading your investments across different asset classes to reduce your overall portfolio's risk. By combining stocks, bonds, and potentially alternative assets, you can create a portfolio that aligns with your individual needs and risk tolerance.

Remember that past performance is not indicative of future results. Thorough research and careful consideration are crucial before investing in any asset class. It’s also essential to remain informed about market trends, economic conditions, and geopolitical events that can affect your investments. Consider seeking professional financial advice to help you create a personalized investment strategy that aligns with your goals and risk profile.

Furthermore, understanding the nuances of investment terminology is crucial for informed decision-making. Terms like "capital appreciation," "yield," "expense ratio," "beta" (a measure of volatility), and "Sharpe ratio" (a measure of risk-adjusted return) are Essential to grasp. Familiarity with these concepts will empower you to critically evaluate different investment options and make informed decisions that align with your financial goals.

For example, let's contrast a high-yield bond with a low-yield bond.

A high-yield bond, also known as a junk bond, offers a higher interest rate to compensate for the increased risk of default. These bonds are typically issued by companies with lower credit ratings, meaning there's a greater chance they might fail to meet their debt obligations. On the other hand, a low-yield bond, such as a government bond, offers a lower interest rate due to its lower risk. The choice between these two depends on your risk tolerance and investment goals. If you're willing to accept higher risk for the potential of higher returns, a high-yield bond might be considered. However, if you prioritize capital preservation and a stable income stream, a low-yield bond might be a more suitable choice.

Similarly, let's compare an actively managed mutual fund with a passively managed index fund. An actively managed fund has a professional fund manager who makes investment decisions aimed at outperforming a benchmark index. However, this comes with higher management fees. A passively managed index fund, on the other hand, simply mirrors a particular market index, such as the S&P 500, at a significantly lower cost. The decision between these two depends on your belief in the ability of active managers to consistently outperform the market. Some investors believe that the higher fees associated with actively managed funds are not justified by the added performance, opting instead for the lower-cost index funds.

In conclusion, navigating the world of investments requires understanding the diverse range of vehicles available and their associated risks and rewards. This understanding, combined with careful planning and ongoing monitoring, will equip you to build a robust and diversified portfolio capable of withstanding economic volatility and achieving your long-term financial goals. Remember that consistent learning and adaptation are key to successful investing in today's dynamic economic landscape.

Diversification Strategies for a Volatile Market

Building a resilient investment portfolio in today's unpredictable economic climate necessitates a proactive and multifaceted approach. While understanding individual asset classes – stocks, bonds, mutual funds, and alternative investments – is crucial, it's equally vital to comprehend how these components interact within a diversified portfolio to mitigate risk and maximize long-term growth. Diversification isn't simply about spreading your money across various asset classes; it's a strategic process tailored to your unique risk tolerance, financial goals, and time horizon.

The core principle of diversification lies in reducing the impact of any single investment's underperformance on your overall portfolio. If one segment of your portfolio experiences losses, the gains from other, more robust segments can help offset those losses, minimizing the overall impact on your wealth. This strategy isn't about eliminating risk entirely – that's impossible in the world of investing – but rather about managing and reducing it to an acceptable level.

A crucial aspect of diversification is asset allocation. This involves determining the proportion of your portfolio dedicated to each asset class (stocks, bonds, real estate, etc.). The optimal asset allocation varies significantly depending on your individual circumstances.

Younger investors with a longer time horizon before retirement generally tolerate higher risk and can allocate a larger portion of their portfolio to stocks, which historically offer higher long-term returns, even if they exhibit greater short-term volatility.

Conversely, investors closer to retirement typically prioritize capital preservation and reduce their exposure to riskier assets, shifting a larger portion of their investments to bonds and other lower-risk instruments.

Consider a hypothetical scenario: A 35-year-old investor with a high-risk tolerance might allocate 70% of their portfolio to stocks (including a mix of large-cap, mid-cap, and small-cap companies across diverse sectors), 20% to bonds (a mix of government and corporate bonds), and 10% to alternative assets such as real estate or gold. This aggressive allocation reflects their longer time horizon and capacity to absorb potential short-term losses in pursuit of higher long-term gains. In contrast, a 60-year-old investor nearing retirement might adopt a more conservative approach, perhaps allocating 40% to stocks, 50% to bonds, and 10% to alternative assets. This allocation prioritizes capital preservation and income generation over aggressive growth.

Beyond the basic asset allocation, effective diversification extends to sector and industry diversification. Concentrating investments within a single sector or industry exposes your portfolio to significant risks if that particular sector underperforms. For instance, an over-reliance on technology stocks could lead to substantial losses if the technology sector experiences a downturn. Therefore, spreading investments across various sectors— technology, healthcare, consumer staples, energy, financials, etc. — is crucial. Within each sector, diversification across different companies minimizes the impact of any single company's failure.

Geographical diversification also plays a critical role. Focusing solely on domestic markets exposes your portfolio to the risks and vulnerabilities of a single economy. Investing in international markets provides diversification benefits by reducing dependence on a single country's economic performance. Emerging markets, while presenting higher risk, offer potential for higher returns and diversification benefits. However, it's important to carefully assess the political and economic stability of these markets before investing.

The methods for evaluating the effectiveness of your diversification strategy are multifaceted. Regular portfolio reviews are essential to ensure your asset allocation aligns with your evolving financial goals and risk tolerance. Analyzing the correlation between

Different assets in your portfolio is equally important. Ideally, your assets should exhibit low or negative correlation, meaning their performance doesn't move in tandem. If your assets are highly correlated (e.g., two technology stocks), a downturn in one is likely to negatively impact the other, negating the diversification benefits. Modern portfolio theory provides mathematical frameworks for optimizing portfolio diversification by considering asset correlation and risk tolerance. Sophisticated investors may utilize advanced tools and software to analyze their portfolios and optimize diversification based on these theoretical models.

Real-world examples highlight the power of diversification. The 2008 financial crisis significantly impacted the financial sector, causing substantial losses for investors heavily invested in financial stocks. However, investors with diversified portfolios, including exposure to other sectors like consumer staples or healthcare, experienced less severe losses as the gains in these sectors offset some of the losses in the financial sector. Similarly, the recent volatility in the technology sector has underscored the need for diversification within the sector itself and across various asset classes. A portfolio over-weighted in technology stocks would have faced significant challenges, while a well-diversified portfolio would have felt the impact to a lesser degree.

Beyond the traditional asset classes, incorporating alternative investments into your portfolio offers additional diversification benefits. These might include real estate, commodities (such as gold, silver, or oil), private equity, and hedge funds. However, it's crucial to acknowledge that alternative investments often have higher entry barriers, lower liquidity, and potentially higher fees compared to traditional assets. They may also require specialized knowledge and expertise to evaluate effectively. Therefore, a careful analysis of your own risk tolerance and financial sophistication is necessary before including alternative investments in your portfolio.

In conclusion, diversification is not a one-time strategy; it's an ongoing process of adaptation and refinement. Regularly reassessing your portfolio's asset allocation, sector exposure, and geographic diversification is paramount to maintaining a resilient and robust investment strategy. The economic landscape is constantly evolving, and your diversification strategy must adapt to these shifts to continue protecting your wealth and maximizing your potential for long-term growth. Professional financial advice can prove invaluable in navigating the complexities of diversification and ensuring your portfolio is strategically aligned with your individual needs and risk appetite. Remember, building wealth is a marathon, not a sprint, and a properly diversified portfolio is your key to navigating the inevitable bumps in the road.

Chapter 2: Navigating the Stock Market

Fundamental analysis forms the bedrock of informed stock investment decisions. It's a process that delves deep into a company's financial health, operational efficiency, and competitive landscape to gauge its intrinsic value and future growth potential. Unlike technical analysis, which focuses on price charts and trading patterns, fundamental analysis examines the underlying fundamentals of a business to determine whether its stock price accurately reflects its true worth. This approach empowers investors to identify undervalued companies with significant growth prospects, minimizing the risk of investing in overvalued or financially precarious entities.

The cornerstone of fundamental analysis lies in understanding and interpreting a company's financial statements. These are the official records that detail a company's financial performance and position. The three primary financial statements are the income statement, the balance sheet, and the statement of cash flows. Each provides a unique perspective on the company's financial health, and a comprehensive analysis requires examining all three in conjunction.

The **income statement,** also known as the profit and loss (P&L) statement, reports a company's revenues, expenses, and resulting net income or loss over a specific period, typically a quarter or a year. By carefully analyzing the income statement, investors can assess a company's profitability, revenue growth trends, and the efficiency of its operations. Key metrics include revenue growth, gross profit margin, operating profit margin, and net profit margin.A consistently growing revenue stream accompanied by healthy profit margins suggests a financially strong and well-managed company. Conversely, declining revenues or shrinking profit margins may indicate underlying problems requiring further investigation. Analyzing the composition of revenues – identifying the contributions of various product lines or services – provides valuable insights into a company's diversification and dependence on specific offerings. Significant reliance on a single product line, for instance, exposes the company to considerable risk if that product loses market share or faces competition.

The **balance sheet** provides a snapshot of a company's assets, liabilities, and equity at a specific point in time. Assets represent what the company owns (cash, accounts receivable, inventory, property, plant, and equipment), while liabilities represent what the company owes (accounts payable, loans, bonds payable). Equity represents the shareholders' stake in the company, calculated as assets minus liabilities. Analyzing the balance sheet allows investors to assess a company's financial strength, liquidity, and solvency. Key ratios derived from the balance sheet, such as the current ratio (current assets divided by current liabilities) and the debt-to-equity ratio (total debt divided by total equity), provide insights into the company's ability to meet its short-term obligations and manage its overall debt burden. A high debt-to-equity ratio, for example, indicates a company is heavily reliant on debt financing, increasing its financial risk.

The **statement of cash flows** tracks the movement of cash into and out of a company over a specific period. It categorizes cash flows into three main activities: operating activities (cash generated from the company's core business operations), investing activities (cash spent on capital expenditures or acquisitions), and financing activities (cash raised through debt or equity financing). Analyzing the statement of cash flows allows investors to assess a company's ability to generate cash from its operations, its investment strategy, and its reliance on external financing. Positive cash flow from operations is a crucial indicator of a healthy and sustainable business. A company that consistently generates positive cash flow even during periods of low profitability demonstrates its strength and resilience. Consistent negative cash flow, on the other hand, warrants careful scrutiny and raises concerns about the company's long-term viability.

Beyond the individual financial statements, fundamental analysis involves calculating and interpreting various financial ratios to gain a more comprehensive understanding of a company's performance and financial health. The **Price-to-Earnings (P/E) ratio,** for instance, compares a company's stock price to its earnings per share (EPS). A high P/E ratio suggests the market is valuing the company's future earnings highly, potentially indicating growth potential but also implying a higher valuation risk. Conversely, a low P/E ratio may indicate undervaluation, but it could also suggest concerns about the company's future prospects. The **return on equity (ROE)** measures the profitability of a company relative to its shareholders' equity. A high ROE indicates efficient use of equity to generate profits. The **debt-to-equity ratio,** as mentioned earlier, reveals the company's reliance on debt financing. The **current ratio** indicates the company's ability to meet its short-term obligations.

It is crucial to remember that financial ratios should not be considered in isolation. Comparing a company's ratios to industry averages and its historical performance provides valuable context and insights. A consistently improving trend in key ratios, even if the absolute values aren't exceptionally high, indicates positive momentum and increasing financial strength. Similarly, a sudden deterioration in key ratios, such as a sharp increase in debt or a significant decline in profit margins, warrants further investigation and caution.

Beyond the quantitative analysis of financial statements and ratios, fundamental analysis also incorporates qualitative factors. This involves considering factors such as management quality, competitive landscape, industry trends, and overall economic conditions. A strong management team with a proven track record, a robust competitive advantage, and a favorable industry outlook are all positive indicators of a company's future prospects. Conversely, a poorly managed company operating in a declining industry faces significant risks.

Analyzing the competitive landscape is crucial. Is the company a market leader or a niche player? Does it possess a sustainable competitive advantage, such as strong brand recognition, proprietary technology, or cost leadership? Understanding the company's position within its industry provides valuable insight into its growth potential and profitability. Industry trends are also vital. Is the industry growing, shrinking, or undergoing significant changes? How is the company adapting to these changes? A company operating in a rapidly growing industry has greater potential for growth, while a company struggling to adapt to industry disruptions faces significant headwinds. Finally, the broader macroeconomic environment also plays a significant role. Interest rates, inflation, and overall economic growth can all have a substantial impact on a company's performance.

Access to reliable data is fundamental for conducting thorough fundamental analysis. Companies themselves provide financial statements through their annual reports (10-K filings) and quarterly reports (10-Q filings) which are available through the Securities and Exchange Commission's (SEC) EDGAR database. Financial news websites and databases like Bloomberg and Refinitiv provide in- depth financial data, industry analysis, and analyst reports. These resources allow investors to access comprehensive information to conduct comprehensive and informed analysis. However, caution is advised; it's always wise to critically assess the source of information and ensure its accuracy and objectivity. Different analysts may interpret the same data differently, leading to divergent conclusions.

Ultimately, fundamental analysis is a multifaceted process requiring a thorough understanding of financial statements, the ability to interpret financial ratios, and a keen awareness of qualitative factors. It's a continuous process, requiring ongoing monitoring and reassessment to incorporate new information and adapt to changing circumstances. By diligently applying the principles of fundamental analysis, investors can significantly improve their chances of identifying undervalued companies with substantial growth potential and mitigate the risk of investing in financially unstable entities. Remember, investing is a long-term endeavor, and consistent effort in analyzing a company's underlying fundamentals is crucial for long-term success.

Technical Analysis for Short-term and Long-term Investing

Technical analysis offers a contrasting approach to fundamental analysis, focusing on price movements and trading volume to predict future price trends. Instead of delving into a company's financial statements, technical analysts study charts and graphs, seeking patterns and indicators that suggest potential buying or selling opportunities. While fundamental analysis provides a snapshot of a company's intrinsic value, technical analysis aims to capitalize on market sentiment and price momentum.

The foundation of technical analysis lies in the interpretation of price charts. These charts visually represent the price of a security over time, often displaying both the price and trading volume.

Several chart types exist, each offering a unique perspective. The most common are:

Line Charts: These charts simply connect the closing prices of a security over a period, providing a clear visual representation of price trends. Line charts are useful for identifying long-term trends but lack the detail of other chart types.

Bar Charts: Bar charts provide more information than line charts, displaying the high, low, open, and close prices for each period (typically a day). The vertical bar visually represents the price range for that period, while the high and low points are marked at the top and bottom of the bar. Bar charts are helpful for understanding price fluctuations within a given period.

Candlestick Charts: These charts are similar to bar charts but provide a more visually intuitive representation of price movements. The "body" of the candlestick represents the difference between the open and close prices, while the "wicks" (or shadows) extend upwards to the high price and downwards to the low price. Candlestick charts are particularly useful for identifying patterns and reversals in price trends.

Regardless of the chart type chosen, analyzing price movements involves identifying key support and resistance levels. Support levels represent price points where the price is expected to find buying pressure and bounce back from, while resistance levels represent price points where selling pressure is anticipated, potentially leading to a price decline. These levels are often formed by previous price highs and lows, creating horizontal lines on the chart. Breakouts above resistance levels can signal bullish trends, while breakdowns below support levels can signal bearish trends.

Technical analysis utilizes a wide range of indicators to identify trends and potential trading opportunities. These indicators mathematically process historical price and volume data to generate signals. Some of the most common indicators include:

Moving Averages: Moving averages smooth out price fluctuations, highlighting underlying trends. The most common are simple moving averages (SMA) and exponential moving averages (EMA). SMAs give equal weight to all data points within the period, while EMAs assign greater weight to recent data points. Crossovers of different moving averages (e.g., a 50-day SMA crossing above a 200-day SMA) are often interpreted as signals of potential trend changes.

Relative Strength Index (RSI): The RSI measures the magnitude of recent price changes to evaluate overbought or oversold conditions. RSI values above 70 are often considered overbought, suggesting a potential price reversal, while values below 30 are often considered oversold, suggesting a potential bounce.

Moving Average Convergence Divergence (MACD): The MACD indicator combines two moving averages to identify momentum changes. The crossover of the MACD line and signal line can signal potential trend changes. Divergences between the MACD and price action can also be important signals.

Bollinger Bands: Bollinger Bands are volatility indicators that plot bands around a moving average. These bands widen during periods of high volatility and contract during periods of low volatility. Prices bouncing off the upper or lower bands can be interpreted as potential reversals.

Technical Analysis for Short-Term Investing:

Short-term trading strategies using technical analysis focus on identifying quick price movements and taking advantage of short- term market fluctuations. Traders may use indicators like RSI and MACD to identify overbought or oversold conditions, aiming to buy at oversold levels and sell at overbought levels. Scalping, a strategy focused on making very short-term trades, often employs technical indicators to identify very short-term price changes. Day traders utilize various charts and indicators to capture intraday price fluctuations. Chart patterns like head and shoulders, double tops, and double bottoms are frequently utilized to anticipate short-term trend reversals. The use of price action trading, which identifies trading opportunities based on direct price movements and candlestick patterns, is also common among short-term traders. Short-term traders must carefully manage their risk, typically using stop-loss orders to limit potential losses. Understanding risk management is paramount for short-term investors, especially considering the volatility of short-term trades.

Technical Analysis for Long-Term Investing:

In contrast to short-term trading, long-term investing with technical analysis focuses on identifying sustained trends and holding investments for extended periods. Long-term investors might employ indicators like moving averages to confirm major trend direction. Breakouts above long-term resistance levels might signal a significant uptrend, while breakdowns below long-term support levels might signal a bearish trend. Long-term investors also pay attention to broader market trends and economic indicators, combining technical analysis with fundamental analysis. While price charts provide a visual representation of market sentiment and price momentum, they need to be considered in the context of the company's financial health and industry position. Long-term investors often look for confirmation of trends from multiple indicators, aiming to minimize false signals. A common strategy for long-term investors is to accumulate positions gradually, adding shares during periods of price dips or consolidation, and adjusting their portfolio based on the confirmed major trend changes supported by multiple indicators.

Combining Technical and Fundamental Analysis:

While technical and fundamental analyses represent different approaches, combining both provides a more holistic perspective for informed investment decisions. Fundamental analysis helps determine a stock's intrinsic value, providing a long-term perspective on its prospects. Technical analysis complements this by identifying optimal entry and exit points, helping to manage risk and time the market. By integrating both, investors can capitalize on short-term trading opportunities while aligning their positions with long-term growth potential. This approach reduces reliance on single indicator signals.

Caveats and Considerations:

It's crucial to acknowledge that technical analysis is not a foolproof method. Markets can be irrational and influenced by various factors beyond the scope of technical indicators. False signals are common, and relying solely on technical analysis can lead to significant losses. It's essential to combine technical analysis with fundamental analysis and sound risk management practices. Additionally, back testing trading strategies and refining your approach over time are crucial to improving your performance. Diversification remains a cornerstone of successful investment, mitigating risks associated with individual stocks.

In conclusion, technical analysis is a valuable tool for both short- term and long-term investors. However, its effectiveness relies on understanding the underlying principles, utilizing multiple indicators, and combining it with other investment strategies. A well-rounded investor employs both fundamental and technical analyses, utilizing various methods to enhance their decision- making process and navigate the complexities of today's markets effectively. Remember, rigorous self-education, ongoing market monitoring, and consistent refinement of your investment strategy are critical for long-term success.

Identifying Promising Stocks with High Growth Potential

Identifying promising stocks with high growth potential requires a multifaceted approach that blends rigorous fundamental analysis with insightful technical analysis and a keen understanding of broader market trends. It's not enough to simply chase the next hot tip; successful long-term investing demands a disciplined, research- driven strategy.

Fundamental analysis forms the bedrock of this strategy. This involves a deep dive into a company's financial health, examining its balance sheet, income statement, and cash flow statement. Look for companies with consistent revenue growth, increasing profit margins, and strong free cash flow. A healthy balance sheet, showing manageable debt levels and ample liquidity, is also crucial. Don't just focus on the headline numbers; delve into the details. Understand the company's business model, its competitive advantages, and its management team's track record. Examine its market share, its growth prospects within its industry, and its ability to innovate and adapt to changing market conditions.

Consider using key financial ratios to assess a company's performance and compare it to its peers. Metrics such as Return on Equity (ROE), Return on Assets (ROA), and Price-to-Earnings (P/E) ratios offer valuable insights into profitability, efficiency, and valuation. However, remember that ratios alone don't tell the whole story; they should be interpreted within the broader context of the company's overall financial health and industry dynamics. Research the company's history, paying attention to its past performance and any significant events that may have affected its trajectory. This historical context can reveal valuable information about the company's resilience and adaptability.

Beyond the financial statements, investigate the company's competitive landscape. Analyze its market position, its competitive advantages, and the potential threats from competitors. A strong competitive moat, such as a unique technology, strong brand recognition, or significant economies of scale, can be a key indicator of long-term growth potential. Examine the industry the company operates within. Is it a growing industry with strong future prospects? Are there any disruptive technologies or trends that could impact the industry's trajectory? A thorough understanding of the industry context is crucial for identifying companies poised for growth.

Once you've conducted a comprehensive fundamental analysis, you can incorporate technical analysis to identify favorable entry and exit points. While technical analysis doesn't reveal a company's intrinsic value, it can help time your investments effectively. Use chart patterns, indicators, and volume analysis to identify potential support and resistance levels, as well as signs of momentum. However, remember that technical analysis is not a crystal ball. Market sentiment can be unpredictable, and even the most sophisticated technical indicators can produce false signals. Therefore, it's essential to combine technical analysis with fundamental analysis and sound risk management practices.

Sector analysis plays a vital role in identifying high-growth industries. Focusing on sectors experiencing rapid growth or technological disruption can significantly increase your chances of finding promising stocks. Emerging sectors such as renewable energy, artificial intelligence, biotechnology, and cloud computing often present attractive investment opportunities, but they also involve higher risks due to their inherent volatility. Thorough research is crucial to understand the underlying dynamics of these sectors and identify companies with a sustainable competitive advantage.

Consider the macroeconomic environment. Interest rates, inflation, and economic growth can significantly impact stock market performance. A strong economy often supports higher stock valuations, while economic downturns can lead to significant market corrections. Understanding the macroeconomic backdrop and its potential influence on specific sectors is important in identifying growth opportunities and mitigating risks.

Examples of successful growth stocks often showcase a combination of strong fundamentals, disruptive innovation, and favorable market conditions. Companies like Amazon, Apple, and Microsoft, for Example, demonstrated consistent revenue and earnings growth, strong brand recognition, and a capacity for innovation. Their success was also fueled by favorable macroeconomic trends and significant technological advancements. Analyzing successful growth stocks can help you identify key characteristics and patterns to look for when screening potential investments.

However, it's crucial to avoid the trap of investing solely based on hype. "Meme stocks" and other speculative investments often attract significant attention but can be highly volatile and subject to rapid price swings. Remember that investing is a long-term game. Don't let short-term market fluctuations derail your long-term strategy. Thorough due diligence is essential. Don't rely solely on online forums or social media for investment advice. Conduct your own research and critically evaluate the information you find.

Diversification is a crucial element of any successful investment strategy. Don't put all your eggs in one basket. Spread your investments across different sectors, industries, and asset classes to mitigate the risk of significant losses. A diversified portfolio can withstand market volatility and provide a more stable long-term return.

Regularly review your portfolio and adjust your strategy as needed. Market conditions change constantly, and your investment approach should adapt to these changes. Periodically reassess your holdings, considering factors such as company performance, industry trends, and macroeconomic developments. Be prepared to sell underperforming assets and re-allocate your capital to more promising opportunities.

Finally, remember that patience and discipline are key to successful long-term investing. Don't be swayed by short-term market noise. Focus on building a diversified portfolio of high-quality stocks, and allow your investments to grow over time. Consistent monitoring, informed decision-making, and a long-term perspective are essential for achieving your financial goals. The path to identifying promising stocks with high growth potential is a journey that requires continuous learning, research, and a disciplined investment approach. Remember to consult with a qualified financial advisor before making any investment decisions, as this information is for educational purposes only and not personalized investment advice.

Understanding Different Stock Classifications Aggressive Medium Aggressive Safe

Understanding the nuances of stock market investment necessitates a clear grasp of risk tolerance and the inherent volatility associated with different asset classes. Within the equity market, stocks are broadly categorized based on their risk profiles – aggressive, medium-aggressive, and safe low-risk. A well-diversified portfolio often incorporates a strategic blend of these classifications to balance potential returns with acceptable levels of risk. This section delves into the characteristics of each category, offering practical insights into how to assess their risk-reward profiles and effectively integrate them into your investment strategy.

Aggressive stocks, also known as growth stocks, are characterized by their high-growth potential and, conversely, high volatility. These companies are typically young, innovative businesses operating in rapidly expanding sectors. Their earnings may be unpredictable, and their share prices can experience significant fluctuations, often exhibiting dramatic swings upwards and downwards. The promise of substantial returns attracts investors willing to accept higher risk. However, the potential for substantial losses is equally significant. Investing in aggressive stocks is generally only suitable for investors with a high risk tolerance and a long-term investment horizon, meaning they can afford to ride out short-term market downturns.

Examples of sectors often associated with aggressive stocks include biotechnology, technology (particularly cutting-edge areas like artificial intelligence and nanotechnology), and renewable energy. Companies within these sectors often lack a long, established track record, making it more challenging to predict their future performance accurately. Their valuation is often based more on future expectations rather than current profitability. While the potential rewards are substantial, the inherent uncertainty necessitates a careful assessment of the company's fundamentals, management team, and market position before investing. Analyzing financial statements, studying industry trends, and assessing competitive advantages become even more crucial when dealing with aggressive stocks. Investing in these stocks should not be impulsive; thorough due diligence is paramount.

Medium-aggressive stocks represent a middle ground between aggressive and safe low-risk investments. These stocks exhibit a moderate level of risk and reward. Companies in this category usually demonstrate consistent growth, although not as rapid as aggressive stocks. They generally possess a more established market position and track record compared to aggressive stocks, offering investors a degree of stability while still offering the potential for above-average returns. Medium-aggressive stocks can be found across various sectors, including established technology companies, consumer discretionary goods, and some industrial businesses. They often offer a blend of growth and value, making them a suitable choice for investors with moderate risk tolerance seeking above-average market returns.

The assessment of medium-aggressive stocks requires a balanced approach. While historical financial performance provides a more reliable gauge than with aggressive stocks, investors should still remain vigilant in analyzing future prospects. Factors such as industry competition, technological disruptions, and macroeconomic conditions can significantly influence the performance of medium-aggressive stocks. Monitoring key financial ratios, such as Price-to-Earnings (P/E) ratios and Return on Equity (ROE), alongside examining industry trends, will aid in making well- informed decisions. Diversification within this category is crucial to mitigate risk. Spread your investments across multiple companies and sectors within this medium-aggressive category to reduce the potential impact of any single company underperforming.

Safe, low-risk stocks are characterized by their relative stability and lower volatility. These stocks are typically issued by large, well- established companies with a history of consistent profitability and dividend payments. These companies are often leaders in their respective industries, possessing strong brand recognition and significant market share. While their growth potential might be lower compared to aggressive or medium-aggressive stocks, they provide a degree of stability and income through dividends, making them suitable for investors with a low risk tolerance or those seeking a steady income stream. Examples include blue-chip companies in sectors like consumer staples, utilities, and pharmaceuticals.

When evaluating safe low-risk stocks, the focus shifts towards consistency and stability. Investors examine historical financial performance, dividend payout ratios, and balance sheet strength. The presence of a strong moat, protecting the company from competition, is a key consideration. Analyzing the company's debt levels and cash flow is crucial to ensure its financial health and ability to continue paying dividends consistently. While these stocks might not deliver exceptional returns, they provide a sense of security and stability in a portfolio, helping to balance out the risks associated with more volatile investments. These stocks act as a buffer during periods of market uncertainty, providing a sense of stability and income in potentially volatile times.

The allocation of investments across these three stock classifications is a deeply personal decision contingent on individual risk tolerance, financial goals, and investment horizon. A younger investor with a longer time horizon may be more inclined towards a higher allocation to aggressive stocks, accepting the higher risk for the potential of greater long-term gains. In contrast, an investor closer to retirement may prefer a more conservative approach, prioritizing capital preservation over high-growth potential, leading them to allocate a larger portion of their portfolio to safe low-risk stocks.

Furthermore, the allocation should be revisited periodically. As personal circumstances change or market conditions shift, it is vital to reassess the risk profile and adjust the allocation accordingly. Regular reviews of the portfolio allow for adapting to changes in risk tolerance and market dynamics, ensuring the portfolio remains aligned with the investor's goals. Remember that the goal isn't just about maximizing returns, but also about achieving them in a manner that is consistent with the investor's individual circumstances and risk appetite.

It's crucial to remember that past performance is not necessarily indicative of future results. While analyzing historical data provides valuable insights, it's essential to factor in future projections and market trends. Emerging technologies, regulatory changes, and shifts in consumer preferences can significantly impact the performance of stocks across all classifications. Therefore, continuous monitoring and a thorough understanding of the market are essential for making well-informed investment decisions. Never invest in a stock based solely on past performance or hype. Conduct thorough research, evaluate all available information, and compare the potential risks and rewards before committing your capital.

Building a diversified portfolio that incorporates a blend of aggressive, medium-aggressive, and safe low-risk stocks is a fundamental aspect of prudent investment management. The specific allocation within these categories should be determined based on individual circumstances and risk tolerance, always remembering the importance of long-term financial goals. Remember that the stock market inherently involves risk. No investment strategy guarantees success, and it's possible to experience losses, even with a well-diversified portfolio. It's imperative to consult with a qualified financial advisor for personalized guidance tailored to your specific circumstances. This information is for educational purposes and should not be considered as personalized investment advice.

Mitigating Risk in Stock Investments

Diversification is a cornerstone of effective risk management in stock investments. It's the principle of spreading your investments across a range of different assets to reduce the impact of any single investment performing poorly. Instead of placing all your eggs in one basket, a diversified portfolio holds assets from various sectors, industries, and even asset classes. This approach aims to lessen the overall volatility of your portfolio and reduce the potential for significant losses. For example, an investor might allocate a portion of their portfolio to technology stocks, another portion to healthcare stocks, and yet another to real estate investment trusts (REITs). If the technology sector experiences a downturn, the losses might be partially offset by gains in other sectors.

The level of diversification needed depends heavily on an individual's risk tolerance and investment objectives. A more conservative investor might opt for a broadly diversified portfolio, spanning multiple sectors and geographies, with a heavier weighting towards established, less volatile companies. A more aggressive investor, aiming for potentially higher returns, might accept more risk and diversify across a wider array of sectors and asset classes, including potentially higher-risk investments like emerging market stocks or small-cap companies. However, even aggressive investors benefit from diversification – it's not about eliminating risk entirely, but about managing it effectively.

Beyond sector diversification, geographical diversification is also crucial. Investing solely in the domestic market exposes your portfolio to the risks specific to that economy. By investing in international markets, you can reduce your reliance on a single economy's performance and potentially increase your returns. For instance, a portfolio concentrated in the US market might suffer significantly during a US recession, while a globally diversified portfolio might experience less severe impacts due to the inclusion of assets from other countries that are less affected.

Diversification extends beyond individual stocks and encompasses asset allocation as a whole. A well-rounded portfolio typically includes various asset classes, not just stocks. Bonds, real estate, commodities (such as gold and silver), and even alternative investments can contribute to a diversified strategy. Bonds, for example, are generally considered less volatile than stocks and can act as a buffer during market downturns, helping to protect your overall portfolio value. Real estate, another relatively low-correlation asset, can offer diversification benefits and a hedge against inflation.

Stop-loss orders offer a proactive approach to risk management. A stop-loss order is an instruction given to your broker to sell a stock when it reaches a predetermined price, thereby limiting potential losses. This order helps to automatically protect your investment if the stock price declines unexpectedly. For example, if you bought a stock at $50 and set a stop-loss order at $45, the stock will be automatically sold if it falls to $45, preventing further losses. While stop-loss orders don’t eliminate risk entirely, they can mitigate the impact of significant price drops.

However, it's crucial to understand that stop-loss orders don't guarantee the exact execution price. Market fluctuations can cause your order to be executed at a price slightly below your stop-loss level. Additionally, stop-loss orders can trigger premature selling during temporary market dips, potentially missing out on subsequent price increases. Therefore, selecting an appropriate stop-loss price requires careful consideration, balancing the need for loss protection with the potential for missing out on gains.

Dollar-cost averaging (DCA) is a strategy that involves investing a fixed amount of money at regular intervals, regardless of the market price. This strategy reduces the risk of investing a lump sum at a market peak, potentially mitigating potential losses. By spreading out your investments over time, you effectively buy more shares when prices are low and fewer shares when prices are high. For example, investing $1000 per month into a stock over a year, regardless of its price, helps to mitigate the risk of timing the market. While DCA doesn't guarantee higher returns, it smooths out the volatility of your investment by reducing the average cost per share. Dollar-cost averaging is particularly beneficial for investors who are unsure about the best time to enter the market. It eliminates the pressure of trying to predict market timing, allowing for a disciplined approach to investing. However, DCA may not yield the highest possible returns if the market consistently trends upwards, as you would miss out on the potential gains from buying at lower prices early on. It's essential to weigh the benefits of reduced risk against the potential for lower overall returns.

Beyond these specific techniques, developing a sound risk management strategy requires a broader perspective. This includes understanding your personal risk tolerance, which is the level of risk you're comfortable taking with your investments. Your risk tolerance will influence your asset allocation and investment choices. A young investor with a long investment horizon might tolerate a higher level of risk, whereas an older investor nearing retirement might prioritize capital preservation and opt for a lower- risk strategy.

Your investment goals also play a vital role in shaping your risk management approach. If your goal is long-term wealth accumulation, you might tolerate higher risk to achieve potentially higher returns. However, if your goal is short-term income generation, a low-risk strategy might be more appropriate. Defining clear, measurable, achievable, relevant, and time-bound (SMART) goals allows you to assess the risk-reward profile of various investment options and make choices aligned with your objectives.

Regular portfolio reviews are crucial for maintaining effective risk management. Your circumstances and market conditions change over time; periodic review allows you to adjust your portfolio accordingly. This might involve rebalancing your asset allocation to maintain your desired risk level, adjusting stop-loss orders, or modifying your investment strategy in response to changes in the market. Regular portfolio reviews are not simply about checking performance; they're about ensuring your investments remain aligned with your goals and risk tolerance.

It's crucial to remember that no investment strategy guarantees success. Market fluctuations are inevitable, and losses are possible even with careful planning and risk management. Therefore, understanding the inherent risks involved in stock investments, developing a robust risk management strategy, and consistently adhering to it are paramount to achieving your long-term financial goals. Consider seeking professional financial advice to build a personalized investment strategy that matches your specific needs and risk tolerance. The information provided here is for educational purposes only and should not be construed as personalized investment advice. Always consult with a qualified financial advisor before making any significant investment decisions.

Chapter 3: Exploring Alternative Investments

Having explored various aspects of traditional stock market investments and risk management strategies, let's turn our attention to alternative investment avenues. A significant portion of a diversified portfolio might include assets that offer a different risk- return profile compared to stocks and bonds. One such category is precious metals, primarily gold and silver. These have historically served as a haven for investors seeking to preserve capital during periods of economic uncertainty or inflation.

Gold, in particular, has held a special place in investment portfolios for centuries. Its inherent value, perceived scarcity, and limited supply have contributed to its enduring appeal as a store of value. Historically, during times of economic turmoil or geopolitical instability, investors often flock to gold as a safe haven asset, driving up its price. This behavior stems from the belief that gold will retain or even increase in value, unlike other assets that might depreciate during such events. The limited supply of gold ensures that its value is not diluted by easy expansion like fiat currencies which can be printed at will.

This safe haven characteristic of gold is supported by considerable historical data. For instance, during the 2008 financial crisis, while many other asset classes experienced significant declines, gold prices surged, demonstrating its ability to act as a hedge against market volatility. Similarly, during periods of high inflation, gold has often shown a positive correlation, preserving purchasing power as the value of fiat currencies erodes. This is because, unlike currencies that are susceptible to inflationary pressures, gold's value tends to appreciate when the general price level rises.

However, it's crucial to acknowledge that gold's performance is not consistently positive. There are times when gold prices decline, and it's not immune to market forces. Factors influencing its price include global economic conditions, currency fluctuations, investor sentiment, and even jewelry demand. A strong US dollar, for example, can negatively impact the price of gold, as it becomes more expensive for investors holding other currencies to purchase it.

Silver, while sharing some characteristics with gold, has a distinct profile as a precious metal investment. Silver is an industrial metal as well, meaning its price is influenced not only by investment demand but also by its industrial applications in various sectors such as electronics, photography, and solar energy. This dual nature makes silver more susceptible to fluctuations than gold, exposing it to the interplay of both precious metal markets and industrial commodity markets. Therefore, silver often experiences more volatility than gold, presenting both greater risk and potentially higher reward opportunities.

Deciding whether to invest in gold or silver, or both, involves considering your individual risk tolerance and investment goals. If you prioritize capital preservation and stability, gold may be a better fit, despite its potential for slower growth. If you are more risk-tolerant and are willing to accept higher volatility for the potential of higher returns, silver might be considered. Moreover, diversification between both assets can help smooth out individual market fluctuations.

Another crucial consideration when investing in precious metals is whether to invest in physical gold and silver or paper gold (like gold ETFs or mutual funds). Purchasing physical gold and silver involves owning the actual metal, which offers tangible ownership and security. This approach, however, necessitates secure storage solutions, which might involve additional costs and logistical considerations. In addition, the purchase and sale of physical gold and silver typically involve transaction costs, like premiums above the spot price.

Paper gold, on the other hand, offers a more convenient and cost- effective method of exposure to the precious metal market. Exchange-traded funds (ETFs) and mutual funds that track gold prices are easily traded, providing investors with liquid access to the market. The transaction costs associated with paper gold investments are often lower than those for physical metals. However, it's critical to understand that you don't directly own the physical metal when investing in paper gold; your investment is based on the fund's value which is directly tied to the underlying price of gold.

Choosing between physical and paper gold depends largely on an investor's investment style and comfort level. Some investors prefer the peace of mind that comes with owning the actual metal, while others find the convenience and efficiency of paper gold more appealing. A balanced approach might involve allocating a portion of your precious metals investment to both physical and paper assets to mitigate the risks associated with each.

The allocation of your investment portfolio to precious metals is a significant decision that requires careful assessment of your personal risk profile, investment objectives, and overall asset allocation strategy. While precious metals can act as a hedge against inflation and market volatility, they do not generate regular income like dividend-paying stocks or interest-bearing bonds. This needs to be considered as part of your overall financial planning. They might not always provide positive returns, requiring a longer- term perspective. Furthermore, the price of precious metals can fluctuate significantly, creating periods of potential gains or losses.

Considering the historical performance and factors influencing the price movements of gold and silver, a well-informed investment strategy would include research into the broader macroeconomic trends. This includes analyzing central bank policies, inflation rates, geopolitical events, and industrial demand for precious metals. Understanding these factors helps to inform your investment decisions.

Finally, it's crucial to consult with a financial advisor before making any significant investments in precious metals or any other asset class. They can assess your risk tolerance and financial goals, aiding in creating an investment strategy that aligns with your circumstances. They can help you determine the optimal allocation of your portfolio to precious metals, ensuring it is consistent with your overall investment objectives and risk tolerance level.

Remember, diversification is key, and precious metals should be viewed as a part of a comprehensive investment strategy, not as a standalone solution. Any investment should be made only after careful consideration and analysis of potential risks and rewards. This chapter aims to provide information for educational purposes and is not financial advice. You must conduct thorough research and seek professional guidance before making any investment decision.

Real Estate Investments Strategies and Considerations

Having explored the intricacies of precious metals as an alternative investment class, we now shift our focus to another significant area: real estate. Real estate investments offer a tangible asset class with the potential for substantial returns, but also come with unique risks and considerations. Unlike stocks or bonds, real estate investments typically require a higher initial capital outlay and involve more hands-on management, particularly in the case of direct property ownership. However, the potential for long-term appreciation, rental income generation, and tax advantages makes it an attractive option for many investors.

One of the primary ways to invest in real estate is through direct property ownership. This involves purchasing residential or commercial properties with the intention of generating rental income, appreciating the property value over time, or both. Direct ownership offers the greatest control over your investment, allowing you to manage every aspect of the property, from tenant selection and rent collection to maintenance and renovations. However, it also demands a significant time commitment and involves the risks associated with property management, including potential vacancies, repairs, and tenant issues. Furthermore, the liquidity of direct real estate investments is relatively low compared to stocks, making it challenging to quickly convert your investment into cash if needed.

The success of a direct property investment hinges on several factors. Location is paramount. Properties situated in desirable neighborhoods with strong rental demand and potential for appreciation tend to perform better than those in less desirable areas. Thorough due diligence is critical, requiring a careful assessment of the property's condition, potential maintenance costs, and local market trends. An accurate assessment of rental rates and potential vacancy periods is equally important in projecting your returns. Understanding local zoning regulations and property taxes is also crucial for managing costs and ensuring compliance.

Financing plays a significant role in the feasibility and profitability of direct property investment. Securing favorable mortgage terms is essential, requiring a good credit score and a demonstrated ability to service the loan. The leverage provided by a mortgage can amplify both gains and losses, making it crucial to carefully assess your capacity to manage the financial risk involved. Understanding the different types of mortgages, interest rates, and repayment schedules is crucial for making an informed decision. An experienced mortgage broker can provide invaluable assistance in navigating the complex world of financing real estate purchases.

Let's consider a real-world example. Imagine an investor purchasing a triplex in a rapidly growing urban area with high rental demand. After thorough research into the local market, property values, and rental rates, the investor secures a mortgage at a favorable interest rate. They carefully select tenants, maintaining the property to a high standard. The investor manages the property effectively, minimizing vacancies and maximizing rental income. In this scenario, the combination of rental income and property appreciation yields a substantial return on investment.

Conversely, imagine an investor purchasing a property in a declining neighborhood with high vacancy rates and significant maintenance issues. The investor struggles to find reliable tenants, faces unexpected repair costs, and ultimately struggles to cover the mortgage payments. In this case, the investment is likely to result in financial losses. The difference highlights the importance of careful due diligence, sound financial planning, and effective property management.

Beyond direct ownership, another popular way to access the real estate market is through Real Estate Investment Trusts (REITs). REITs are companies that own, operate, or finance income- generating real estate. They are publicly traded, making them more liquid than direct property investments. REITs offer diversification benefits, as they often hold a portfolio of properties across various sectors and locations. They also typically distribute a significant portion of their income to shareholders in the form of dividends, providing a steady stream of passive income.

There are various types of REITs, including equity REITs, which own and operate income-producing properties; mortgage REITs, which finance real estate investments; and hybrid REITs, which combine both equity and mortgage investments. The choice of REIT depends on your investment goals and risk tolerance. Equity REITs generally offer higher potential for capital appreciation, but also carry higher risk. Mortgage REITs are generally considered less risky, but offer lower potential returns. Diversifying across different types of REITs can help mitigate risk and enhance potential returns.

Investing in REITs offers several advantages, including liquidity, diversification, and dividend income. However, the performance of REITs can be influenced by various factors, including interest rate changes, economic conditions, and the performance of the underlying real estate market. REITs are also subject to market fluctuations, meaning their prices can go up or down, affecting the value of your investment.

Another related approach is through investment in real estate investment funds (or private equity funds focused on real estate). These typically involve pooled investments, managed by professionals, offering exposure to a diversified portfolio of properties or development projects. Access to these funds often requires higher minimum investment levels, and liquidity may be limited compared to publicly traded REITs. However, professional management can help to mitigate some of the risks and complexities associated with direct real estate investment. It's also crucial to understand the specific investment strategy and associated fees of these private investment vehicles.

Careful analysis of a fund's track record, management team, and investment strategy is essential before investing. Transparency and clear communication from the fund managers are key to understanding the investment process and associated risks.

Regardless of the chosen investment strategy – direct ownership, REITs, or real estate funds – a thorough understanding of market dynamics is crucial. Understanding factors such as local market conditions, interest rates, rental trends, and economic forecasts helps in making informed investment decisions. Analyzing comparable properties, considering potential appreciation, and assessing the overall risk-return profile are all integral parts of a robust investment strategy.

It's imperative to remember that real estate investments, like any other investment, are not without risks. Market fluctuations, economic downturns, unexpected maintenance costs, and difficulties in finding or managing tenants can all impact returns. A well-diversified portfolio, coupled with a comprehensive understanding of the risks and potential rewards of each investment option, is essential for long-term success. Furthermore, seeking professional advice from a real estate specialist or financial advisor is highly recommended before making any substantial real estate investment. This guidance can help tailor an investment strategy that aligns with your individual financial goals and risk tolerance. Remember, this information is for educational purposes only and not financial advice. Conduct thorough research and seek professional guidance before making any decisions.

Cryptocurrencies and other Digital Assets

Having explored the complexities of real estate investment, we now turn our attention to a rapidly evolving and often volatile asset class: cryptocurrencies and other digital assets. This area presents both significant opportunities and considerable risks, demanding a thorough understanding before considering any investment.

At its core, the foundation of most cryptocurrencies lies in block chain technology – a decentralized, distributed ledger that records and verifies transactions across a network of computers. This eliminates the need for a central authority, such as a bank or government, to oversee transactions, making the system theoretically more transparent and secure. Each transaction is cryptographically secured and added to a block, which is then linked to the previous block, forming a chain. This "chain" of blocks is publicly accessible, ensuring the integrity and immutability of the data. The decentralized nature of block chain contributes to its resilience against censorship and single points of failure.

Bitcoin, the first and arguably most well-known cryptocurrency, operates on this principle. However, thousands of other cryptocurrencies, or altcoins, have since emerged, each with its unique characteristics and functionalities. These altcoins often aim to improve upon Bitcoin's limitations or provide different functionalities, such as enhanced transaction speeds, smart contract capabilities, or decentralized finance (DeFi) applications.

The price of cryptocurrencies is notoriously volatile, subject to rapid and significant fluctuations. Several factors contribute to this volatility. Firstly, the relatively small market capitalization compared to traditional asset classes means that even modest trading volumes can lead to substantial price swings. Secondly, cryptocurrency prices are heavily influenced by market sentiment, news events, regulatory developments, and technological advancements. A positive news story can trigger a surge in price, while negative news can lead to a dramatic sell-off. Furthermore, the lack of intrinsic value, unlike traditional assets like real estate or commodities, makes cryptocurrency prices largely dependent on speculation and market psychology.

Regulatory uncertainty also plays a crucial role. Governments worldwide are still grappling with how to regulate cryptocurrencies, with approaches varying significantly across different jurisdictions. This lack of clear regulatory frameworks can create uncertainty and volatility in the market, impacting investor confidence and price stability. Changes in regulatory landscape, even the anticipation of such changes, can lead to significant price movements.

Technological advancements within the cryptocurrency space also influence prices. Innovations such as improved scalability solutions, the development of new consensus mechanisms, and the introduction of DeFi applications can all impact the perceived value and adoption rate of a particular cryptocurrency. Conversely, technological vulnerabilities or security breaches can lead to significant price drops, as witnessed in several instances in the past.

Understanding the various types of cryptocurrencies is crucial for informed investment. Beyond Bitcoin, Ethereum has emerged as a major player, offering a platform for decentralized applications (dApps) and smart contracts. Smart contracts are self-executing contracts with the terms of the agreement written directly into code, automating various processes and agreements. Numerous other altcoins cater to specific niches or functionalities, such as privacy coins, which prioritize user anonymity, or stable coins, which aim to maintain a relatively stable price compared to fiat currencies like the US dollar.

Investing in cryptocurrencies requires a high risk tolerance. The potential for substantial returns is undeniable, but so is the potential for significant losses. The highly speculative nature of the market means that investors need to be prepared for significant price fluctuations and the possibility of losing a portion or even all of their investment. Unlike traditional assets with established valuation methods, the valuation of cryptocurrencies remains subjective and depends heavily on market sentiment.

Due diligence is paramount before investing in cryptocurrencies. Thoroughly research the specific cryptocurrency you are considering, understanding its underlying technology, use case, development team, and market capitalization. Evaluate its potential for growth and adoption, while acknowledging the inherent risks and volatility. Diversification across different cryptocurrencies can help mitigate some of the risk, but it does not eliminate the possibility of losses.

Security is another critical consideration. Cryptocurrency exchanges and wallets can be vulnerable to hacking and theft, so selecting reputable and secure platforms is essential. Use strong passwords, enable two-factor authentication, and be wary of phishing scams. Storing your cryptocurrencies in a secure hardware wallet can further enhance security, reducing the risk of unauthorized access.

Furthermore, it is important to understand the tax implications of cryptocurrency investments. The tax treatment of cryptocurrencies varies significantly depending on the jurisdiction, with potential implications for capital gains tax, income tax, and other tax liabilities. Seeking advice from a qualified tax professional is crucial to ensure compliance with all applicable regulations.

Beyond cryptocurrencies, the broader digital asset landscape encompasses other investment opportunities. Non-fungible tokens (NFTs) represent unique digital assets, often representing ownership of digital artwork, collectibles, or in-game items. The value of NFTs is often driven by scarcity, community demand, and brand recognition. However, the NFT market is also highly speculative, subject to significant price volatility and potential for fraud.

Security tokens, another type of digital asset, are often tied to real- world assets, such as stocks, bonds, or real estate. They represent fractional ownership of an underlying asset and can offer enhanced liquidity and transparency compared to traditional investment vehicles. However, the regulatory landscape surrounding security tokens is still evolving, creating potential uncertainty and risk.

Investing in cryptocurrencies and other digital assets is not suitable for all investors. It requires a deep understanding of the technology, market dynamics, and associated risks. Only invest what you can afford to lose, and never invest based solely on hype or speculation. Diversification, thorough research, and a long-term perspective are crucial for navigating this volatile yet potentially rewarding asset class. Furthermore, consider seeking advice from a financial advisor experienced in alternative investments before making any decisions, ensuring your investment strategy aligns with your overall financial goals and risk tolerance. Remember, this information is for educational purposes only and is not financial advice. Always conduct thorough independent research and consult with a professional before investing.

Analyzing the Potential of Emerging Markets

Having considered the intricacies of cryptocurrencies and digital assets, we now shift our focus to another exciting, yet equally complex, realm of alternative investments: emerging markets. Specifically, we will delve into the burgeoning sectors of artificial intelligence (AI) and electronics/chip manufacturing, exploring the immense potential they offer alongside the inherent risks involved.

The allure of emerging markets lies in their potential for exponential growth. These sectors are often characterized by rapid innovation, disruptive technologies, and a first-mover advantage for early investors. However, this high-growth potential comes with increased volatility and uncertainty. Unlike established markets with mature business models and predictable revenue streams, emerging markets are inherently more speculative, making rigorous due diligence absolutely critical.

The AI sector, arguably one of the most transformative technological advancements of our time, presents a multitude of investment opportunities. AI is rapidly permeating various aspects of our lives, from healthcare and finance to transportation and manufacturing. Companies developing AI algorithms, software, and hardware are experiencing significant growth, attracting substantial investment from both public and private sources. However, it is essential to distinguish between genuine innovation and hype-driven speculation within the AI space.

Identifying promising AI companies requires a keen understanding of the underlying technologies. Consider companies specializing in machine learning, deep learning, natural language processing, or computer vision. Analyze their competitive advantages, intellectual property portfolio, and the potential market size for their products or services. Moreover, assess the quality of their management team, their track record, and their financial health. A company with strong fundamentals, a clear roadmap, and a sustainable competitive advantage is far more likely to deliver long-term returns than a company driven solely by market hype. For instance, a company pioneering advancements in medical AI diagnostics could potentially revolutionize healthcare, leading to substantial revenue growth. Conversely, a company focused on a niche AI application with limited market potential might struggle to achieve significant returns. It's crucial to evaluate the specific application of AI, its scalability, and its potential impact on the respective market. Due diligence should include analyzing market research reports, industry publications, and expert opinions to gain a holistic understanding of the company's prospects.

The electronics/chip manufacturing sector is another key player in the emerging market landscape. The global demand for semiconductors and integrated circuits continues to rise exponentially, fueled by the growth of the computing, communications, and automotive industries. Companies involved in the design, manufacturing, and distribution of these essential components are poised for significant growth, particularly those companies focusing on leading-edge technologies.

However, the semiconductor industry is characterized by high capital expenditures, complex manufacturing processes, and intense competition. Companies operating in this sector must continuously invest in research and development to maintain a competitive edge. Moreover, geopolitical factors, such as trade wars and supply chain disruptions, can significantly impact the profitability of semiconductor companies.

Analyzing the potential of a chip manufacturing company requires an understanding of its manufacturing capabilities, its technology node, its customer base, and its market share. A company possessing advanced manufacturing capabilities, a strong customer base, and a dominant market position is likely to be better positioned for growth than a company with limited capabilities and a small market share.

For example, a company specializing in the production of cutting- edge chips used in high-performance computing could benefit from the growing demand for artificial intelligence, high-performance computing, and 5G technologies. However, a company producing older generation chips might struggle to compete in a rapidly evolving market. Therefore, assessing the technological competitiveness of the company and its ability to adapt to future technological shifts is paramount.

Beyond individual companies, macroeconomic factors significantly influence the performance of emerging markets. Interest rates, inflation, exchange rates, and geopolitical events can all impact the growth prospects of these sectors. For instance, rising interest rates can make it more expensive for companies to borrow money, potentially hindering their expansion plans. Similarly, geopolitical instability can disrupt supply chains and negatively impact business operations.

Diversification is essential when investing in emerging markets. Investing in multiple companies across different sub-sectors within AI and electronics/chip manufacturing can mitigate some of the risks associated with individual company performance. Furthermore, diversifying across geographies can reduce exposure to country-specific risks.

Thorough due diligence is not just a suggestion; it's an absolute necessity when considering investments in emerging markets. This includes a meticulous analysis of the company's financial statements, industry trends, competitive landscape, and management team. Access to reliable and up-to-date information is paramount, utilizing a combination of financial databases, industry reports, and news sources.

Furthermore, understanding the regulatory environment is crucial. Government regulations, particularly in technology-related sectors, can significantly impact the growth and profitability of companies. Changes in regulatory frameworks can create both opportunities and challenges for investors. Therefore, staying abreast of evolving regulatory landscapes is vital for making informed investment decisions.

Finally, patience is a virtue when investing in emerging markets. These sectors are prone to periods of high volatility, with significant price fluctuations in the short term. A long-term perspective, focusing on the company's fundamental strengths and its long-term growth potential, is essential for weathering market fluctuations and realizing long-term returns. Avoid impulsive decisions driven by short-term market trends, and always remember the importance of a well-defined investment strategy aligned with your risk tolerance and overall financial goals. Remember, this information is for educational purposes and does not constitute financial advice. Always seek professional guidance before making any investment decisions.

Diversifying Across Asset Classes

Diversification is the cornerstone of sound investment strategy, a principle as fundamental as the need for a well-structured financial plan. While the allure of high-growth potential in emerging markets like AI and semiconductor manufacturing is undeniable, relying solely on these sectors exposes your portfolio to significant risk. A truly robust investment strategy necessitates spreading your capital across a variety of asset classes, each with its own unique characteristics and risk profile. This strategic allocation minimizes the impact of downturns in any single asset class, enhancing the overall resilience and long-term growth potential of your portfolio.

Consider a portfolio heavily weighted in technology stocks. While the tech sector has historically delivered impressive returns, periods of correction can be sharp and severe. A diversified portfolio, however, would incorporate other asset classes, such as bonds, real estate, and commodities, which may perform differently during periods of market volatility. This diversification acts as a buffer, mitigating the impact of losses in the technology sector and potentially even generating gains from other positively performing assets.

The most common asset classes include stocks, bonds, and cash equivalents. Stocks represent ownership in a company and offer the potential for high growth, but also carry higher risk. Bonds, on the other hand, are debt instruments issued by governments or corporations, offering a fixed income stream with lower risk compared to stocks. Cash equivalents, such as money market accounts and certificates of deposit (CDs), provide liquidity and stability but typically offer lower returns.

Within each asset class, further diversification is crucial. Instead of investing in a single stock, a well-diversified equity portfolio would include a variety of stocks across different sectors, market capitalizations, and geographies. Similarly, a bond portfolio would include bonds with varying maturities, credit ratings, and issuers. This approach reduces the impact of any single company or sector underperforming, safeguarding the overall portfolio's performance. Real estate provides another compelling diversification opportunity. Historically, real estate has shown a relatively low correlation with stocks and bonds, meaning its price movements tend to be independent of those in the stock and bond markets. This lack of correlation can be advantageous during market downturns, as real estate might hold its value or even appreciate while other assets decline. Real estate investment can take various forms, from directly owning properties to investing in real estate investment trusts (REITs), which offer exposure to a diversified portfolio of real estate assets without the direct responsibilities of property ownership. However, real estate investments are often illiquid, meaning they can be challenging to sell quickly without potentially accepting a lower price.

Alternative investments, as discussed previously, represent a broader category encompassing assets outside of traditional stocks, bonds, and real estate. This includes commodities like gold and silver, which are often considered safe haven assets during times of economic uncertainty. Private equity and hedge funds also fall under this umbrella, providing access to investment strategies not readily available in public markets. While these alternatives can offer attractive returns and diversification benefits, they typically come with higher risks and require specialized knowledge and experience. Access is often limited to accredited investors with significant net worth. Furthermore, alternative investments might be illiquid, meaning they may be difficult to quickly convert to cash.

The allocation of your portfolio across various asset classes should be carefully considered based on your individual circumstances, risk tolerance, and financial goals. Younger investors with a longer time horizon might tolerate higher risk and allocate a larger portion of their portfolio to equities, aiming for higher growth potential. Older investors closer to retirement, however, may prefer a more conservative approach, allocating a larger portion to bonds and cash equivalents to preserve capital and generate income.

A common approach to asset allocation is to utilize a strategic asset allocation model, where the portfolio's target allocations to various asset classes are determined based on risk tolerance and financial goals. These allocations are then regularly rebalanced to maintain the desired target allocation. This systematic rebalancing helps to capitalize on market fluctuations, selling some of the better- performing assets and reinvesting the proceeds in underperforming ones, potentially enhancing overall portfolio returns.

However, it is important to recognize that market conditions are dynamic, requiring flexibility in investment strategies. A tactical asset allocation approach involves adjusting the portfolio's allocations based on short-term market forecasts and economic conditions. This approach requires a higher degree of market expertise and may involve more frequent trades. While potentially lucrative, it is critical to understand that market forecasts can be inaccurate, and tactical asset allocation carries a higher risk of losing capital compared to strategic asset allocation.

Let's illustrate the benefits of diversification with a hypothetical example. Imagine two investors, Investor A and Investor B, both with $100,000 to invest. Investor A invests solely in technology stocks, while Investor B diversifies their portfolio across stocks, bonds, and real estate. In a scenario where the technology sector experiences a significant downturn, Investor A's portfolio could suffer substantial losses. However, Investor B's diversified portfolio might experience some losses in the stock portion, but the gains in the bond and real estate segments could partially offset these losses, resulting in a more moderate decline overall. Conversely, in a scenario where the technology sector booms, Investor A would see substantial gains. But Investor B, despite potentially missing out on the full upside in the tech sector, would still enjoy significant gains, while enjoying some stability from the less volatile bonds and real estate segments of the portfolio.

The practical application of diversification involves a detailed understanding of your own risk tolerance. Are you comfortable with higher volatility in pursuit of potentially higher returns, or do you prioritize capital preservation? A financial advisor can assist you in determining your risk profile through various questionnaires and discussions. This assessment is critical in making informed decisions about your asset allocation strategy, ensuring that your investments are aligned with your overall financial objectives.

Furthermore, actively managing your portfolio is an ongoing process, requiring continuous monitoring and adjustment as your circumstances change. Regular rebalancing, as mentioned earlier, is key in maintaining your target allocation. Staying informed about macroeconomic trends and market conditions is also crucial to making informed adjustments to your portfolio. Consider utilizing various financial news sources, industry reports, and engaging with your financial advisor for guidance.

The creation of a diversified portfolio should not be approached as a one-time event but as a dynamic process tailored to your individual financial circumstances and goals. It necessitates consistent monitoring, adjustments, and adaptability to changing market dynamics. Remember to always seek the guidance of a qualified financial advisor before making any significant investment decisions. They can provide personalized recommendations based on your specific situation, help you navigate complex investment options, and ensure that your investment strategy remains consistent with your long-term financial plan. The complexities of the financial markets necessitate a well-structured plan and an understanding of the critical role diversification plays in achieving your financial aspirations.

Chapter 4: Retirement Planning Strategies

Planning for retirement involves more than simply saving money; it requires a strategic approach to accumulating and managing assets to secure your financial future. A cornerstone of this strategy is choosing the right retirement accounts. Understanding the various options available, and selecting the ones best suited to your individual circumstances, is crucial for maximizing your retirement savings and minimizing tax burdens. Let's delve into the most common retirement account options, examining their benefits, drawbacks, and how they might fit into your overall financial plan.

One of the most prevalent retirement savings vehicles is the 401(k) plan. Sponsored by employers, these plans allow employees to contribute a portion of their pre-tax salary, reducing their taxable income in the present. The contributions are often matched, at least partially, by the employer, providing an immediate boost to your savings. The power of employer matching cannot be overstated; it's essentially free money that significantly accelerates the growth of your retirement nest egg. Many 401(k) plans also offer a range of investment options, from low-risk bonds and money market funds to higher-risk stocks and mutual funds. The flexibility in investment choices allows you to tailor your portfolio to your risk tolerance and long-term financial objectives. However, 401(k) plans often have limitations on investment choices compared to individual Retirement accounts (IRAs), and some plans may charge higher fees than others. Furthermore, access to your funds before retirement is typically restricted, with penalties applied for early withdrawals.

Another widely used retirement plan is the traditional IRA (Individual Retirement Account). Unlike 401(k)s, IRAs are not Employer-sponsored. Individuals can contribute to an IRA regardless of whether or not their employer offers a retirement plan.

Contributions made to a traditional IRA are tax-deductible, reducing your taxable income for the year. However, the Distributions in retirement are taxed as ordinary income. The contribution limits for traditional IRAs are set annually by the IRS, and there are income limitations for deducting contributions fully. For example, high-income earners may face restrictions on the amount they can deduct. This differs from 401(k)'s where income levels do not directly impact contribution limits (although some plans may have maximum contribution levels). Traditional IRAs offer greater investment flexibility than many 401(k) s, allowing for a wider range of investments including stocks, bonds, mutual funds, and even some alternative investments. They also provide more control over investment management compared to employer-sponsored plans.

A significant alternative to the traditional IRA is the Roth IRA. Roth IRAs differ fundamentally from traditional IRAs in their tax treatment. Contributions to a Roth IRA are not tax-deductible, meaning you contribute after-tax dollars. However, the significant Advantage lies in tax-free withdrawals in retirement. This means that your withdrawals and earnings accumulate tax-free, potentially leading to a larger nest egg compared to a traditional IRA, especially in higher tax brackets later in life. Similar to traditional IRAs, Roth IRAs have annual contribution limits set by the IRS, and there are income limitations that restrict the eligibility to fully contribute to the plan. The eligibility criteria for a Roth IRA can sometimes limit participation for individuals with higher incomes. For example, in certain years, single filers making above a certain income threshold may not be able to make full contributions or contribute at all.

Choosing between a traditional IRA and a Roth IRA is a crucial decision that hinges on your current and projected future tax brackets. If you anticipate being in a higher tax bracket in retirement than you are currently, a Roth IRA might be more advantageous. The tax-free withdrawals in retirement would outweigh the disadvantage of contributing after-tax dollars now. Conversely, if you expect to be in a lower tax bracket in retirement, a traditional IRA with tax-deductible contributions could prove more beneficial. Tax implications depend greatly on individual circumstances, financial predictions and potential future changes in tax legislation. Professional guidance from a financial advisor is strongly recommended to assess the optimal path based on your specific circumstances.

Annuities represent another option for retirement planning, though they function quite differently from 401(k) s and IRAs. Annuities are contracts with insurance companies that provide a stream of income during retirement. There are two primary types: fixed annuities and variable annuities. Fixed annuities offer a guaranteed rate of return, providing a predictable income stream, albeit typically lower compared to other investment options. Variable annuities, on the other hand, offer the potential for higher returns but also carry greater risk, as the returns are tied to the performance of underlying investments. Annuities can provide security and peace of mind, especially for those seeking a consistent income stream in retirement. However, they often come with high fees and surrender charges, which can significantly impact overall returns. Annuities are a complex financial product and require careful consideration of their features and implications before investment. Understanding the fees, surrender penalties and the specific terms of the annuity contract is crucial.

Maximizing your contributions to these various retirement accounts is paramount to building a comfortable retirement. For 401(k) s, contributing up to the maximum amount allowed is often advantageous due to employer matching. For IRAs, contributing the maximum amount annually can significantly accelerate your savings. Careful planning and a disciplined approach to savings is essential to make the most of these retirement savings vehicles.

Let's consider some illustrative examples. A young professional starting their career might prioritize a Roth IRA due to their low current income and potential for higher future earnings. The tax-free withdrawals in retirement would be particularly beneficial in their higher income years. An older individual nearing retirement, however, might choose a traditional IRA to reduce their current tax burden. The tax deduction on contributions would be valuable given their immediate tax bracket. A self-employed individual might rely heavily on a SEP IRA (Simplified Employee Pension Plan) or a Solo 401(k) due to their lack of an employer-sponsored plan. The flexibility provided by these plans allows for self-directed Investments based on their risk appetite.

The selection of the best retirement plan, or combination of plans, depends significantly on your individual financial situation, risk tolerance and your longer-term financial goals. This decision- making process requires a meticulous assessment of your income, age, tax bracket and your anticipated retirement lifestyle. Consider the long-term implications of each choice before making a decision and seek professional advice where necessary. The complexity of tax laws and the market can necessitate the input of a qualified financial professional, who can help you navigate the decision- making process and align your retirement investments with your overall financial objectives. Remember, retirement planning is a continuous process that should be adapted and adjusted over time as your financial circumstances and goals evolve.

Strategies for Maximizing Retirement Savings

Building a substantial retirement nest egg requires more than just contributing to a retirement account; it demands a proactive and multifaceted approach. This involves not only careful selection of the right investment vehicles, as discussed previously, but also diligent budgeting, strategic saving techniques, and exploring avenues to increase your income. The earlier you begin this process, the more powerfully compound interest works in your favor, exponentially increasing your savings over time. Let's explore these crucial strategies in detail.

One of the most fundamental steps is creating a realistic budget. Many individuals underestimate the power of careful budgeting in achieving their financial goals. A well-structured budget meticulously tracks income and expenses, identifying areas where spending can be reduced and savings increased. Start by listing all sources of income—salary, investments, side hustles—and then meticulously categorize all expenses. This often reveals surprising spending patterns, highlighting areas ripe for improvement. For example, tracking daily coffee purchases or dining-out habits can quickly demonstrate the significant cumulative cost of these seemingly small expenses over a year, sometimes amounting to thousands of dollars that could be redirected to your retirement savings. Budgeting apps and software can significantly aid in this process, providing automated tracking and insightful analysis of spending patterns. Remember that budgeting isn't about deprivation; it's about mindful spending, allowing you to allocate more resources toward your long-term financial security.

Once a comprehensive budget is in place, the next step is establishing a consistent savings plan. Automate your savings by setting up automatic transfers from your checking account to your retirement accounts. This ensures regular contributions without requiring constant manual intervention. Even small, regular contributions accumulate substantially over time due to the magic of compound interest. Consider setting a savings goal, such as saving a specific percentage of your income each month or aiming to increase your savings by a certain amount annually.

Regularly reviewing and adjusting your savings plan ensures it aligns with your evolving financial situation and retirement goals.

Beyond consistent saving, optimizing your investment strategy within your retirement accounts is crucial for maximizing returns. This goes beyond simply choosing the right account type (traditional IRA, Roth IRA, 401(k), etc.). It involves actively managing your portfolio to ensure it aligns with your risk tolerance and investment timeline. For instance, younger investors with a longer time horizon can generally tolerate more risk and can allocate a larger portion of their portfolio to equities (stocks), which historically offer higher returns over the long term. Conversely, individuals closer to retirement should adopt a more conservative approach, shifting toward lower-risk investments like bonds and fixed-income securities to protect their accumulated savings. Regularly rebalancing your portfolio is essential to maintain your desired asset allocation, ensuring you don't become overly concentrated in any particular sector or asset class.

Furthermore, diversification is key to mitigating risk. Don't put all your eggs in one basket. Diversify your investments across various asset classes (stocks, bonds, real estate, etc.) and sectors to reduce the impact of any single investment's underperformance. Consider investing in index funds or ETFs (Exchange-Traded Funds), which offer instant diversification across a broad range of stocks or bonds. These low-cost options provide access to a diversified portfolio without requiring extensive research and individual stock picking.

Beyond maximizing your retirement savings through careful budgeting and investment strategies, exploring ways to increase your income can significantly accelerate the process. This might involve seeking a promotion or raise in your current position, negotiating a better salary at a new job, or developing additional streams of income through part-time work, freelancing, or investing in side businesses. Evaluate your skill set and identify potential opportunities to generate supplemental income. The extra income can be directly channeled into your retirement accounts, rapidly boosting your savings. The extra income, even if modest, makes a surprising difference over time when consistently added to your retirement savings. The power of starting early cannot be overstated. Compound interest, the snowball effect of earning interest on both your principal and accumulated interest, is significantly more powerful over longer periods. A small contribution started early can grow exponentially over several decades. For illustrative purposes, let's consider two individuals: Person A starts saving $500 per month at age 25, while Person B starts saving the same amount at age 45. Assuming an average annual return of 7%, Person A will accumulate a substantially larger retirement nest egg by the time they reach 65, illustrating the profound impact of starting early. This is not to discourage later starters; every contribution counts, regardless of age. However, an earlier start leverages the power of compounding to a far greater degree.

To further illustrate the practical application of these strategies, consider several real-world scenarios. A young couple, both in their early thirties and starting their careers, can benefit significantly from maximizing their contributions to Roth IRAs while focusing on budgeting and debt reduction. The tax advantages of a Roth IRA are particularly valuable considering their likely increasing tax bracket in later years. As their income grows, they can increase their savings contributions and explore additional income streams through side hustles or investments. For a self-employed individual, meticulously tracking business expenses for tax optimization is crucial. They might also consider establishing a SEP IRA or a Solo 401(k) to maximize their retirement contributions. An individual approaching retirement might focus on consolidating their assets, rebalancing their portfolio to a more conservative allocation, and potentially exploring annuity options for a guaranteed income stream.

Retirement planning is not a one-time event but a continuous process requiring adaptation as circumstances and goals change. Regularly reviewing your budget, investment strategy, and income streams is crucial to ensure alignment with your evolving financial situation and retirement objectives. Economic downturns, market fluctuations, and unforeseen events might necessitate adjustments to your plan. Remember to seek professional financial advice periodically to review your progress, fine-tune your strategy, and ensure your financial goals remain achievable. The journey to a secure retirement requires a disciplined, proactive, and adaptable approach that incorporates budgeting, strategic saving, optimized investing, and exploration of additional income sources. The rewards of meticulous planning and consistent effort are a comfortable and secure retirement.

Planning for Retirement Income

Planning for retirement income is a critical component of overall retirement planning. It's not enough to simply accumulate savings; you need a well-defined strategy for converting those savings into a reliable stream of income that sustains your desired lifestyle throughout retirement. This requires careful consideration of several key factors, beginning with accurately estimating your future expenses.

Estimating your retirement expenses is arguably the most important step. Many people underestimate their needs, leading to insufficient savings and potential financial hardship in retirement. Start by creating a detailed list of your current expenses, categorized by necessities (housing, food, utilities, and healthcare) and discretionary spending (travel, entertainment, hobbies). Then, project these expenses forward, accounting for inflation. Inflation erodes the purchasing power of money over time, so the same amount of money will buy less in the future than it does today. You can use online inflation calculators to project future expenses more accurately. Consider factors like potential healthcare costs, which tend to increase significantly with age. Also, remember that your lifestyle might change in retirement—you might travel more or engage in more hobbies, potentially increasing expenses. It's prudent to overestimate your expenses rather than underestimate them.

Once you have a reasonable estimate of your retirement expenses, the next step is to determine your potential sources of retirement income. This usually involves a combination of several sources, and it's crucial to understand the implications of each.

Social Security benefits form a vital cornerstone of retirement income for many. However, the amount you receive depends on your earnings history and the age at which you begin collecting benefits. Understanding the complexities of Social Security is crucial. Delaying your benefit collection until your full retirement age or beyond results in higher monthly payments, but you need to weigh this against the risk of not living long enough to recoup the benefits of delayed payments. Explore the Social

Security Administration's website for detailed information on benefit calculations and claiming strategies.

Pensions, if applicable, represent another significant income stream for some retirees. However, traditional defined benefit pension plans are becoming less common. If you are fortunate enough to have a pension, understand the terms of your plan, including payment amounts, payout schedules, and any potential adjustments for cost- of-living increases.

Investment income forms a critical component of most retirement plans. Your investment portfolio, accumulated through years of savings and contributions to retirement accounts like 401(k) s and IRAs, will be the primary source of income during retirement. Your withdrawal strategy during retirement must be carefully planned to avoid depleting your savings too quickly. Several strategies exist, including the constant percentage withdrawal method (withdrawing a fixed percentage of your portfolio each year), the systematic withdrawal plan, and the bucket strategy (allocating assets into separate "buckets" for different time horizons). The most appropriate strategy depends on your risk tolerance, investment portfolio composition, and longevity expectations.

Annuities can provide a guaranteed income stream for life or a specified period, offering a degree of financial security. However, annuities typically involve fees and surrender charges, which can reduce the overall return. Carefully evaluate the costs and benefits before purchasing an annuity. Immediate annuities provide a regular income stream immediately upon purchase, while deferred annuities offer a future income stream. The choice between an immediate or deferred annuity depends on your individual financial situation and retirement timeline.

Reverse mortgages allow homeowners to access their home equity as a source of income, but it's a complex financial product with potential risks. The interest accrues on the loan, and the loan balance increases over time. Reverse mortgages should be carefully considered and fully understood before being utilized. It's essential to seek professional financial advice before taking out a reverse mortgage.

Real estate investments, such as rental properties, can provide a supplemental income stream during retirement. However, managing rental properties requires time, effort, and expertise. The risk of vacancy and maintenance costs must be carefully assessed.

Part-time work or consulting can provide additional income during retirement, supplementing other sources. This approach allows retirees to maintain a sense of purpose while earning extra income to cover expenses or pursue hobbies.

Creating a sustainable retirement plan that accounts for inflation and longevity risk is essential. Regularly reviewing and adjusting your retirement income plan is crucial. Market fluctuations, unexpected expenses, and changes in health conditions may require adjustments to your withdrawal strategy. Consider regularly consulting with a financial advisor to ensure your plan remains viable and meets your changing needs.

The decision of when to begin withdrawing from your retirement accounts is a critical one. Beginning withdrawals too early can deplete your savings prematurely, leaving you with insufficient funds in later years. Delaying withdrawals too long can reduce the overall value of your retirement savings due to inflation. There is no one- size-fits-all answer, but careful consideration of your individual circumstances, life expectancy, and risk tolerance is crucial. Professionals can help you model various withdrawal scenarios and help determine the most appropriate strategy.

Taxes play a significant role in retirement income planning. Understanding the tax implications of different income sources and withdrawal strategies is essential. For instance, withdrawals from traditional IRAs are taxable as ordinary income, while withdrawals from Roth IRAs are generally tax-free. Consult with a tax advisor to develop a tax-efficient withdrawal strategy.

Throughout the process, regular review and adjustments are crucial. Economic downturns, market fluctuations, and unexpected health issues can significantly impact your retirement income. Periodically review your plan with a financial advisor, adjusting your withdrawal strategy, asset allocation, and income sources as necessary to ensure a comfortable and secure retirement. The aim is not simply to survive retirement financially, but to thrive, enjoying the fruits of years of diligent planning and prudent financial management. A well-structured, adaptable plan gives you the freedom to enjoy this next phase of your life with peace of mind.

Tax Implications of Retirement Planning

Understanding the tax implications of your retirement planning is crucial for maximizing your retirement income and minimizing your tax burden. Retirement isn't just about accumulating savings; it's about strategically managing those savings to ensure a comfortable and financially secure future while navigating the complexities of tax laws. This section will dissect the tax ramifications of various retirement plans and investment strategies, providing you with the knowledge necessary to make informed decisions.

Let's start with the fundamental difference between tax-deferred and tax-advantaged accounts. Tax-deferred accounts, such as traditional 401(k)s and traditional IRAs, allow you to contribute pre-tax dollars, reducing your taxable income in the present. This lowers your current tax liability, offering immediate tax savings. However, you'll pay income taxes on your withdrawals in retirement. The tax rate you pay in retirement may be different from your current tax bracket – a crucial consideration. For instance, if your income is significantly lower in retirement than during your working years, your tax bracket may be lower, resulting in a smaller tax burden on your withdrawals. Conversely, if your retirement income is higher than anticipated, including from multiple sources, you may find yourself in a higher tax bracket than you were during your working years.

Tax-advantaged accounts, such as Roth 401(k)s and Roth IRAs, work differently. Contributions to Roth accounts are made after taxes, meaning you don't receive an immediate tax break. However, qualified withdrawals in retirement are tax-free. This structure becomes particularly advantageous if you anticipate being in a higher tax bracket in retirement than you are now. The tax benefits of a Roth account become more pronounced over time as your investments grow tax-free.

The decision of whether to contribute to a tax-deferred or tax- advantaged account is a personal one, dependent on your individual circumstances, income levels, and projected tax brackets during both your working years and retirement. A comprehensive financial plan should take into account your current and projected tax situations to help you choose the most advantageous strategy. Consulting a financial advisor specializing in retirement planning and tax optimization can provide invaluable guidance in making this crucial decision.

Beyond the choice of account type, the specific investment strategies within these accounts also carry tax implications. For example, the sale of stocks held in a taxable account generates capital gains taxes, which are taxed differently depending on the holding period (short-term vs. long-term). Understanding these distinctions is vital for optimizing your tax efficiency. Long-term capital gains, held for more than one year, generally face lower tax rates than short-term capital gains. This incentivizes long-term investing and strategic asset allocation. Tax-loss harvesting, a strategy involving selling losing investments to offset capital gains, can significantly reduce your tax liability. This requires careful planning and understanding of tax rules, but it can be a powerful tool for minimizing your overall tax burden.

Consider the complexities of Required Minimum Distributions (RMDs) for traditional retirement accounts. Once you reach a certain age (currently 75 for those born in 1960 or later, and 73 for those born in 1951-1959), you are required to begin taking annual withdrawals from your traditional IRAs and 401(k)s. These withdrawals are subject to income tax, regardless of your overall income level. Failure to take these RMDs can result in significant penalties. This is another area where careful financial planning and professional advice are essential to ensure compliance and minimize tax liabilities. Furthermore, the RMD calculation itself can be complex, varying depending on the account balance and other factors. Professional help with this can ensure you are adhering to all applicable regulations.

The tax implications of withdrawals extend beyond the distinction between tax-deferred and tax-advantaged accounts. The source of your retirement income influences the taxes you will pay. For instance, Social Security benefits are subject to taxation depending on your combined income from other sources. If your income exceeds certain thresholds, a portion or all of your Social Security benefits may be taxed. This is a significant factor to consider when planning your retirement income strategy. An accurate projection of total income, including Social Security, pensions, and investment income, is crucial for estimating your overall tax liability in retirement.

Pensions, while providing a steady stream of income, may also have tax implications. Some pensions are tax-deferred, meaning payments are taxed as ordinary income upon receipt. Others might be partially or fully taxed depending on how the plan is structured. Understanding the tax status of your pension is critical for accurate budget planning. It's advisable to review your pension plan documents carefully, or seek clarification from the plan administrator, to fully understand the tax ramifications of your pension payments.

Withdrawal strategies from your retirement accounts have significant tax consequences. For instance, systematically withdrawing a consistent percentage of your portfolio each year might simplify budgeting, but it may not optimize your tax situation. A more sophisticated approach, perhaps involving a financial advisor, may consider withdrawing from tax-advantaged accounts first to minimize taxable income in specific years. A personalized withdrawal strategy should be developed in consultation with a tax professional who can factor in individual circumstances and specific tax rules to create a tax-efficient retirement income plan.

Estate planning also integrates seamlessly with tax implications during retirement. Understanding the tax consequences of inheriting retirement accounts is important for both the account holder and beneficiaries. Beneficiaries inheriting traditional IRAs, for example, may be subject to RMDs, influencing their income tax liability. Similarly, rules governing the transfer of Roth IRAs to beneficiaries differ and will influence tax outcomes. Careful estate planning, considering beneficiaries and inheritance, is critical to minimizing estate taxes and ensuring the smooth transfer of assets to heirs.

In conclusion, the tax implications of retirement planning are multifaceted and complex. This is not an area to navigate alone. Seeking professional advice from a qualified financial advisor and tax professional is crucial to developing a comprehensive and tax- efficient strategy that aligns with your individual circumstances and financial goals. A well-structured retirement plan considers not only the accumulation of savings but also the strategic management of those savings throughout retirement to minimize tax liabilities and maximize your after-tax income. This proactive approach ensures you can enjoy a comfortable and financially secure retirement, free from unnecessary tax burdens. The complexity of tax laws necessitates professional guidance to ensure you're not leaving money on the table and are making informed decisions that best serve your long-term financial well-being.

Estate Planning and Legacy Considerations

Estate planning is often overlooked in the excitement of accumulating assets for retirement, but it's a critical component of ensuring your financial legacy and providing for your loved ones. A well-structured estate plan protects your assets, minimizes potential tax liabilities, and ensures your wishes regarding the distribution of your wealth are carried out efficiently and effectively after your passing. This is not simply about creating a will; it's a comprehensive strategy that incorporates several key elements.

One of the foundational elements of estate planning is the creation of a will. A will is a legal document that outlines how your assets will be distributed after your death. Without a will, your assets are distributed according to the laws of intestacy in your state, which may not align with your wishes. This process can be lengthy, complicated, and potentially lead to disputes among family members. A will allows you to specifically name beneficiaries for your assets, including your retirement accounts, bank accounts, real estate, and other personal property. You can also name a guardian for minor children, if applicable.

However, a will alone may not be sufficient for complex estates. For those with substantial assets or complex family situations, a trust can provide additional protection and control. There are various types of trusts, each serving different purposes. Revocable living trusts allow you to maintain control over your assets during your lifetime and modify the trust as needed. Upon your death, the trust assets are distributed according to your instructions. Irrevocable trusts, on the other hand, offer more significant asset protection and tax benefits, but you relinquish control over the assets once the trust is established. The choice between a revocable and irrevocable trust depends heavily on individual circumstances and financial goals, and requires careful consideration with legal and financial professionals.

Beneficiary designations on your retirement accounts, life insurance policies, and other assets supersede your will. This means that regardless of what your will stipulates, the named beneficiaries on these accounts will receive the assets. It's crucial to regularly review and update these beneficiary designations to reflect changes in your family circumstances, such as marriage, divorce, or the birth or death of a child. Failing to update these designations can result in unintended consequences and potentially leave your loved ones without the financial support you intended.

Beyond wills and trusts, proper estate planning also involves the management of potential estate taxes. Estate taxes are levied on the value of your estate upon your death, exceeding a certain threshold. These tax rates can be substantial, significantly diminishing the inheritance received by your heirs. Effective estate planning strategies aim to minimize estate taxes through various methods, including the utilization of trusts, charitable gifting, and strategic asset allocation. Understanding the applicable estate tax laws in your jurisdiction is paramount. The tax laws are complex and frequently change, making professional guidance indispensable.

Furthermore, careful consideration should be given to the implications of long-term care. The costs associated with long-term care, whether in a nursing home or through in-home assistance, can be substantial and rapidly deplete savings. Long-term care insurance can be a valuable tool to mitigate these potential financial burdens. However, the choice of a suitable policy requires a careful evaluation of your individual needs and financial capacity. It's vital to understand the coverage options, limitations, and cost implications before making a decision.

Power of Attorney is another crucial aspect of estate planning. A Power of Attorney designates someone you trust to manage your financial and legal affairs should you become incapacitated. This ensures someone can handle your bills, manage your investments, and make necessary decisions on your behalf if you are unable to do so yourself. This is particularly important in preventing potential financial exploitation and ensuring continuity of your affairs during periods of illness or disability. It's essential to choose someone reliable and trustworthy to fulfill this important role. The document should clearly define the scope of authority granted to the designated individual. Healthcare directives, such as living wills and advance healthcare directives, are essential components of estate planning that address your wishes concerning medical treatment if you are unable to communicate your preferences. A living will outlines your wishes regarding life-sustaining treatment, while a durable power of attorney for healthcare designates someone to make medical Decisions on your behalf. These documents provide clarity and peace of mind, ensuring your wishes are respected in the event of a medical emergency or incapacitation. It's essential to clearly articulate your preferences and ensure these documents are legally sound and up-to-date.

Incorporating digital assets into your estate plan is a relatively new yet vital aspect for modern planning. This encompasses online accounts, social media profiles, digital photographs, and other forms of online data. Many individuals overlook the need to plan for the distribution or deletion of these assets. A comprehensive estate plan should address this aspect to ensure the proper handling and distribution of digital assets. This often involves providing explicit instructions to your designated executor or trustee on how to manage your digital accounts and content.

The process of estate planning can be complex and often requires the expertise of multiple professionals. Consulting with a qualified estate planning attorney is crucial to ensure your plan is legally sound and reflects your wishes accurately. They can help you navigate the intricacies of wills, trusts, and other legal instruments, tailoring a plan to meet your unique circumstances. A financial advisor can assist in developing a strategy to minimize tax liabilities and effectively manage your assets. Working with both these professionals allows for a coordinated and holistic approach to estate planning, ensuring your assets are protected and distributed according to your intentions.

The importance of regular review and updates to your estate plan cannot be overstated. Life circumstances change—marriage, divorce, the birth or death of family members, changes in asset ownership—all necessitate reviewing and updating your estate plan. A periodic review, ideally at least every three to five years, or after significant life events, is recommended to ensure your plan remains current and reflects your current wishes and financial situation. Failing to regularly update your plan can lead to unintended consequences and necessitate costly legal rectification later.

In conclusion, while retirement planning focuses primarily on accumulating sufficient assets to fund your retirement years, estate planning ensures the preservation and distribution of those assets according to your wishes. This comprehensive process involves creating a will or establishing a trust, designating beneficiaries, managing estate taxes, addressing long-term care concerns, and documenting your healthcare preferences. By proactively addressing these matters, you secure your financial legacy, provide for your loved ones, and gain peace of mind knowing your wishes will be carried out effectively and efficiently. The expertise of legal and financial professionals is invaluable in navigating this complex process and ensuring a robust and comprehensive estate plan. Don't delay; start planning your legacy today. The peace of mind gained from a well-structured plan is invaluable.

Chapter 5: Managing Debt and Building Financial Security

Having established a solid foundation for your financial future through prudent investment and comprehensive estate planning, we now turn to a critical aspect of financial security: managing debt. High-interest debt, particularly from credit cards and payday loans, can quickly erode your financial stability and hinder your progress towards retirement goals. This section provides a roadmap to navigate this challenging landscape, offering practical strategies to regain control of your finances.

The first step in tackling high-interest debt is a frank assessment of your current financial situation. This involves creating a detailed budget that meticulously tracks all income and expenses. Many budgeting apps and software programs are available to simplify this process, offering features like automated expense categorization and insightful visualizations of your spending patterns. Identifying areas where you can reduce expenses is crucial. This might involve cutting back on non-essential spending, such as dining out, entertainment, or subscriptions, or finding more cost-effective alternatives for essential expenses like groceries or transportation. This level of detail helps pinpoint areas where adjustments can bring immediate relief.

Once you have a clear understanding of your income and expenses, you can accurately determine your debt-to-income ratio. This ratio is a key indicator of your financial health, showing the percentage of your income that is allocated to debt payments. A high debt-to- income ratio indicates potential financial stress and highlights the urgent need for debt management strategies. There are online calculators readily available that can quickly calculate your debt-to- income ratio, providing a quantifiable measure of your financial standing.

Once you have a comprehensive budget in place, prioritize your debts. One effective method is the debt avalanche method, where you focus on paying off the highest-interest debt first, regardless of the balance. This approach minimizes the total interest paid over the long term, leading to faster debt reduction. Alternatively, the debt snowball method involves paying off the smallest debt first, regardless of the interest rate. While this method may not be the most mathematically efficient, the psychological boost of quickly eliminating a debt can provide motivation to continue the process. The choice between these methods depends on your personal preferences and motivational needs.

Debt consolidation can be a powerful tool for managing multiple debts. This involves combining several high-interest debts into a single loan with a lower interest rate. Several options exist, including personal loans, home equity loans, and balance transfer credit cards. Each option has its own set of requirements and advantages and disadvantages. Personal loans often offer fixed interest rates and predictable monthly payments, while home equity loans use your home's equity as collateral. Balance transfer credit cards typically offer a promotional period with a low or 0% interest rate, but be mindful of the balance transfer fees and the subsequent interest rate after the promotional period ends. Careful comparison of interest rates, fees, and repayment terms is crucial in selecting the best debt consolidation strategy.

Balance transfers can provide immediate relief from high interest charges, particularly if you can secure a card with a 0% introductory APR. However, it's crucial to have a plan for repaying the balance within the promotional period to avoid a sudden spike in interest payments when the introductory rate expires. Paying more than the minimum payment during the promotional period can significantly reduce the total interest paid and expedite debt elimination. Always review the terms and conditions of the balance transfer carefully before proceeding, paying close attention to any transfer fees and the interest rate after the promotional period ends.

For individuals struggling to manage their debt, a debt management plan (DMP) can offer valuable support. Credit counseling agencies provide guidance and negotiate lower interest rates and monthly Payments with your creditors. A DMP consolidates your debt payments into a single monthly payment, making it easier to track and manage. While a DMP can significantly reduce stress and simplify debt management, it will impact your credit score. This negative impact is temporary, however, and is generally outweighed by the benefits of getting your debt under control.

Negotiating with your creditors directly can also yield positive results. Many creditors are willing to work with borrowers facing financial hardship and may offer reduced interest rates or extended repayment periods. Clearly explaining your financial situation and proposing a realistic repayment plan can significantly improve your chances of success. Documenting all communication with creditors is essential for maintaining a record of the negotiation process.

In addition to formal strategies, minor adjustments to your lifestyle can make a big difference. For instance, prioritizing needs over wants, reducing impulsive purchases, utilizing coupons, and exploring free or low-cost entertainment options can help free up funds for debt repayment. These smaller savings, when consistently implemented, contribute to faster debt reduction and improved financial health.

Seeking professional help from a credit counselor is highly advisable if you find yourself overwhelmed by debt. Certified credit counselors provide unbiased guidance and support, helping you create a personalized debt management plan. They can negotiate with creditors on your behalf and offer valuable advice on budgeting, financial literacy, and improving your credit score. Many non-profit credit counseling agencies offer free or low-cost services, ensuring accessibility for individuals facing financial difficulties.

In conclusion, managing high-interest debt requires a multifaceted approach combining budgeting, debt prioritization, consolidation strategies, negotiation, and, when necessary, professional guidance.By adopting a proactive and disciplined approach, you can overcome the challenges of high-interest debt and pave the way for a more secure and prosperous financial future. Remember that the journey towards financial freedom often requires patience and persistence, but the rewards of financial stability and peace of mind

are immeasurable.

Building an Emergency Fund

Building a robust emergency fund is not merely a good financial practice; it's a cornerstone of financial security, acting as a critical buffer against life's unpredictable events. Without this safety net, even minor unexpected expenses can quickly spiral into debt, derailing your carefully crafted financial plans and potentially jeopardizing your retirement goals. This section will guide you through the process of establishing a substantial emergency fund, emphasizing practical strategies and real-world examples to illustrate its crucial role in safeguarding your financial well-being.

The first step in building your emergency fund involves setting realistic, achievable savings goals. Instead of aiming for an unrealistic, overly ambitious target that might lead to discouragement, begin by defining a manageable goal. A commonly recommended starting point is three to six months' worth of living expenses. This amount should cover essential costs like housing, utilities, groceries, transportation, and debt repayments. For example, if your monthly expenses total $3,000, your initial emergency fund goal should be between $9,000 and $18,000. However, this is a baseline; depending on your individual circumstances, a larger fund might be more appropriate. Factors to consider include job security, health status, and the presence of dependents. If you have a less stable job or higher healthcare costs, aiming for a larger emergency fund—perhaps eight to twelve months' worth of expenses—offers greater security.

Once you've set your savings goal, the next critical step is to automate your savings. Most banks and financial institutions offer automated transfer services, allowing you to automatically transfer a predetermined amount from your checking account to your savings account on a regular schedule (weekly, bi-weekly, or monthly). This eliminates the need for manual transfers, reducing the likelihood of forgetting to save and ensuring consistent Contributions to your emergency fund. The power of automation lies in its consistency; small, regular contributions accumulate over time to reach your savings goal, making the process less daunting. Even seemingly insignificant amounts, such as $50 or $100 per Month, can make a substantial difference when compounded over several months or years.

Another effective strategy is to identify potential sources of emergency funds beyond your regular savings. This could include a high-yield savings account, which offers a higher interest rate than a standard savings account, allowing your savings to grow faster. Consider certificates of deposit (CDs), which provide a fixed interest rate for a specific period, offering a predictable return on your investment. While CDs typically have penalties for early Withdrawal, they are suitable for funds you anticipate not needing immediate access to. High-yield savings accounts and CDs represent relatively low-risk, safe investment options that complement your emergency fund.

Beyond traditional savings vehicles, explore other avenues to supplement your emergency fund. For instance, many individuals underestimate the value of their existing assets. Do you have unused gift cards or store credit? These could provide a quick infusion of cash in an emergency. Consider selling items you no longer use or need, such as electronics, clothes, or furniture. Online marketplaces and consignment shops provide convenient platforms for selling used items, potentially generating substantial funds to add to your emergency fund. This approach not only adds to your savings but also declutters your home, offering a double benefit.

Let's illustrate the importance of an emergency fund with a few real-world examples. Imagine a scenario where your car breaks down unexpectedly, requiring a costly repair or replacement. Without a sufficient emergency fund, you might be forced to resort to high-interest loans or credit cards, incurring substantial debt that could take years to repay. Similarly, an unexpected medical expense, such as a hospital stay or major surgery, can quickly deplete your savings if you lack a robust emergency fund. Unexpected job loss is another significant event that highlights the necessity of an emergency fund. In such circumstances, your emergency fund provides crucial financial breathing room, allowing you to cover your living expenses while searching for new employment, reducing the pressure to accept any job hastily just to survive. However, building an emergency fund is not simply about accumulating a large sum of money; it's also about developing responsible financial habits. It's about cultivating a proactive mindset, anticipating potential financial challenges, and preparing accordingly. By consistently contributing to your emergency fund, you're demonstrating a commitment to your financial future, showcasing discipline and a long-term perspective. This discipline extends beyond just saving; it permeates your overall financial approach, influencing your spending habits and investment decisions.

In addition to the practical strategies mentioned above, fostering a mindful approach to spending is crucial. Track your expenses diligently, identifying areas where you can reduce unnecessary spending. This exercise not only frees up funds for your emergency fund but also provides valuable insights into your spending patterns, fostering greater financial awareness. Consider adopting a budgeting app or software to track your finances automatically, offering insightful visualizations of your spending and providing actionable recommendations. This level of financial awareness empowers you to make informed decisions about your spending, ultimately improving your financial management skills.

Regularly reviewing your emergency fund is equally important. Assess its current balance in relation to your evolving expenses and goals. As your income increases or your expenses change, adjust your savings targets accordingly. This continuous review ensures that your emergency fund remains an effective safety net, adapting to changes in your financial circumstances. A regular review also instills financial discipline, reinforcing the importance of maintaining a sufficient emergency fund.

Furthermore, consider regularly reassessing your risk tolerance and adjust your emergency fund accordingly. If you anticipate a period of greater financial uncertainty, perhaps due to a potential job change or an upcoming large expense, bolster your emergency fund to provide a greater level of financial security. This proactive approach mitigates potential financial risks, reducing the likelihood of unexpected financial hardship. Finally, remember that building an emergency fund is a marathon, not a sprint. Progress may seem slow at times, especially during periods of unexpected expenses or financial setbacks. However, persistence and consistent effort are key to achieving your savings goals. Celebrate milestones along the way, acknowledging the progress you've made and maintaining your motivation. The peace of mind that comes with a substantial emergency fund is a significant reward for your efforts. It's an investment in your financial security, providing a crucial buffer against life's uncertainties and paving the way for a more secure and prosperous future. This security enables you to focus on your long-term financial goals, knowing that you have a reliable safety net to fall back on in times of need. By building a solid emergency fund, you are not merely preparing for unforeseen events; you are building a foundation for lasting financial stability and peace of mind.

Protecting Your Assets with Insurance

Having established a robust emergency fund as a cornerstone of your financial security, we now turn our attention to another crucial element: insurance. Insurance acts as a vital shield, Protecting your assets and financial well-being from the unexpected blows life can deliver. While an emergency fund addresses immediate, short-term needs, insurance provides long-term protection against catastrophic events that could otherwise devastate your finances.

Let's begin with health insurance, arguably the most critical form of insurance for most individuals. The costs associated with medical emergencies, chronic illnesses, and long-term care can be astronomical, quickly depleting even the most substantial savings. Health insurance provides a financial safety net, covering a significant portion of medical expenses, preventing you from being burdened with crippling debt. The type of health insurance you need will depend on your individual circumstances, including your age, health status, and employment situation. Employer-sponsored plans are a common source of health coverage, often offering a range of options with varying premiums and deductibles. If you're self- employed or don't have access to employer-sponsored insurance, you'll need to explore individual health insurance plans available through the marketplace or directly from insurance providers. Understanding the intricacies of health insurance plans—premiums, deductibles, co-pays, and out-of-pocket maximums—is crucial to selecting a plan that suits your budget and health needs. Carefully compare plans based on these factors to find the best value.

Beyond health insurance, life insurance plays a crucial role in protecting your loved ones' financial future. In the event of your untimely death, life insurance provides a financial safety net for your dependents, ensuring they can maintain their lifestyle and meet their financial obligations. There are two main types of life insurance: term life insurance and whole life insurance. Term life insurance provides coverage for a specific period, typically 10, 20, or 30 years, at a fixed premium. It's a cost-effective option for those seeking temporary coverage, particularly during periods when financial responsibility for dependents is high. Whole life insurance, on the other hand, provides lifelong coverage with a cash value component that grows over time. While more expensive than term life insurance, whole life insurance offers a combination of death benefit and a savings element. The choice between term and whole life insurance depends on your individual needs and financial goals. Consider factors such as the length of time you need coverage, your budget, and your long-term financial objectives.

Disability insurance is another often-overlooked but critically important form of protection. Disability can strike unexpectedly, leaving you unable to work and generate income. Disability insurance replaces a portion of your lost income, allowing you to maintain your financial stability during a period of incapacitation. There are two main types of disability insurance: short-term and long-term. Short-term disability insurance typically covers a period of a few months, while long-term disability insurance can provide coverage for years or even until retirement. Many employers offer short-term disability insurance as part of their benefits package, but long-term disability insurance is often purchased independently. The benefits of disability insurance are substantial, ensuring financial security during a time of vulnerability. Without disability insurance, an unexpected illness or injury can quickly lead to financial ruin.

Long-term care insurance is another crucial element often neglected in financial planning. Long-term care can be incredibly expensive, encompassing nursing home stays, assisted living facilities, and in- home care. Long-term care insurance helps cover these costs, ensuring that you don't deplete your savings or rely on family members for financial support. The cost of long-term care insurance varies based on factors like your age, health status, and the level of coverage you choose. It's essential to consider purchasing long-term care insurance at a younger age, as the premiums are significantly lower. Delaying the purchase can dramatically increase the cost, making it unaffordable for many. The peace of mind that comes with long-term care insurance is invaluable, knowing that your financial security is protected in the event of a debilitating illness or injury.

Beyond these fundamental types of insurance, consider other forms of coverage relevant to your specific circumstances. Homeowners or renters insurance protects your property and possessions from damage or theft. Auto insurance is mandatory in most states and protects you from financial liability in the event of an accident. Umbrella insurance provides additional liability coverage beyond what's offered by your homeowners or auto insurance policies, offering an extra layer of protection against significant lawsuits. The type and level of coverage you need will depend on your assets, lifestyle, and risk tolerance.

Choosing the right insurance coverage requires careful consideration and planning. Compare policies from different insurers, paying attention to premiums, deductibles, coverage limits, and exclusions. Don't hesitate to consult with an independent insurance agent who can help you navigate the complexities of insurance and find the best coverage for your specific needs. Remember that insurance isn't just about mitigating risk; it's about safeguarding your financial future and providing peace of mind. It's an investment in your security, ensuring that unforeseen events don't derail your long-term financial goals.

Let's illustrate the importance of insurance with some real-world examples. Consider the case of a family whose home is destroyed by a fire. Without homeowners insurance, they would face catastrophic financial losses, potentially losing their home, possessions, and facing significant debt rebuilding their lives. Or imagine an individual who becomes severely injured in a car accident and is unable to work. Without disability insurance, they would face mounting medical bills and a loss of income, leading to financial hardship. These scenarios highlight the crucial role insurance plays in protecting against unexpected events and maintaining financial stability. The cost of insurance is a small price to pay compared to the potential financial devastation of an uninsured event.

Insurance is not a one-size-fits-all solution. The optimal insurance portfolio will vary greatly depending on factors such as age, income, family status, assets, and risk tolerance. Younger individuals with fewer assets might prioritize health insurance and Life insurance, while older individuals with substantial assets might focus on long-term care insurance and umbrella liability coverage.

A comprehensive financial plan should incorporate a thorough review of your insurance needs and regularly re-evaluate your coverage as your circumstances evolve. Regularly reviewing your policies ensures that your coverage remains adequate to meet your changing needs and protects against potential gaps in protection.

In conclusion, integrating a comprehensive insurance strategy into your financial plan is an essential step towards securing your financial future. While building an emergency fund addresses short- term uncertainties, insurance offers a long-term shield against potentially devastating events. By thoughtfully selecting and maintaining appropriate insurance coverage—health, life, disability, long-term care, and others as needed—you safeguard your assets, protect your family, and provide yourself with the peace of mind that comes with knowing you're financially prepared for the

Unexpected. This proactive approach allows you to focus on achieving your long-term financial goals, secure in the knowledge that you've taken the necessary steps to protect yourself and your loved ones from financial hardship. The cost of insurance is a small price to pay for the peace of mind and financial security it provides.

Remember, this is an investment in your future, not an expense.

Understanding and Utilizing Credit Wisely

Understanding and utilizing credit wisely is a cornerstone of building a strong financial foundation. Credit, while a powerful tool when used responsibly, can quickly become a crippling burden if mishandled. This section delves into the mechanics of credit, emphasizing the importance of building and maintaining a good credit score, and offering practical strategies for navigating the complexities of the credit world.

First, let's define credit. Credit is essentially borrowing money with the agreement to repay it over time, usually with interest. This borrowed money can be used for a variety of purposes, from purchasing a home or car to covering unexpected expenses. Your creditworthiness, or your ability to repay borrowed funds, is evaluated by credit bureaus, who assign you a credit score based on your credit history. This score is a numerical representation of your credit risk, with higher scores indicating lower risk and vice- versa. Lenders use this score to assess whether to grant you credit and at what interest rate.

Building a good credit history takes time and responsible behavior. The most important factor influencing your credit score is your payment history. Consistently making your payments on time, whether it's credit card bills, loan payments, or utility bills, is crucial for establishing a positive credit history. Late payments or missed payments significantly damage your credit score, making it harder to obtain credit in the future and increasing the interest rates you'll face. Aim for a goal of making all payments at least a week before the due date to build a history of responsible behavior and avoid even the possibility of being late.

Beyond payment history, the amount of credit you use relative to your available credit, known as your credit utilization ratio, is another key factor influencing your credit score. Keeping your credit utilization low, ideally below 30%, demonstrates responsible credit management. High credit utilization suggests you're heavily reliant on credit, increasing your perceived risk to lenders. For example, if you have a credit card with a $10,000 limit, try to keep Your balance below $3,000. Paying down balances regularly, ideally aiming for zero balances on all revolving accounts monthly, signals responsible credit management.

The length of your credit history also plays a significant role in your credit score. A longer credit history, demonstrating consistent responsible credit use over time, is generally viewed more favorably by lenders. Avoid closing older credit accounts, as doing so can shorten the length of your credit history, potentially harming your score. This is even true if you don't use the card regularly, so you may even consider using those older accounts for small monthly transactions to maintain their active status. This doesn't require excessive spending, but a minimal purchase and prompt payment helps maintain their positive status.

The types of credit you utilize also impact your credit score. A mix of different credit accounts, such as credit cards, installment loans, and mortgages, demonstrates a broader range of credit experience and can positively influence your score. However, avoid opening too many new credit accounts in a short period, as this can be seen as a sign of potential financial instability and can negatively impact your credit score. Each credit application results in a hard inquiry on your credit report, which can temporarily lower your score. Apply only when necessary and avoid unnecessary applications for credit cards or loans.

Maintaining a good credit score is an ongoing process. Regularly monitoring your credit report and score is essential to identifying any errors or potential problems. You are entitled to a free credit report from each of the three major credit bureaus (Equifax, Experian, and TransUnion) annually. Review your reports carefully and dispute any inaccuracies immediately. A single incorrect entry can significantly impact your credit score, potentially affecting your ability to secure loans or other forms of credit. Be aware of identity theft and fraud that can appear on your credit reports. Regularly checking your report is a proactive measure to help protect yourself from these events.

Understanding the different types of credit is also crucial for making informed financial decisions. Credit cards are revolving

Credit accounts, meaning you can borrow up to your credit limit repeatedly, provided you make the minimum payments. Installment loans, on the other hand, are loans with a fixed repayment schedule over a set period, such as auto loans or personal loans. Mortgages are long-term installment loans used to finance the purchase of a home. Each type of credit has its own advantages and disadvantages, and the best choice for you will depend on your specific needs and financial situation. Be certain to understand the terms and interest rates associated with all forms of credit before agreeing to them. This is especially true with more exotic financial instruments that are not widely understood.

Using credit responsibly is vital for maintaining good financial health. Avoid accumulating high-interest debt, as this can quickly spiral out of control and lead to financial hardship. Make a budget, sticking to your limits so you're not living beyond your means, and prioritize paying down high-interest debt as quickly as possible. Explore options for debt consolidation if you're struggling to manage multiple debts, and always prioritize paying on time, even in difficult situations, to preserve your credit rating.

Avoiding common credit pitfalls is essential for preserving your financial well-being. One common mistake is applying for too many credit cards or loans in a short period. This negatively impacts your credit score, and it can be challenging to recover from this. Another is failing to read and understand the terms and conditions of credit agreements. Take the time to review all of the fine print, even if it seems tedious. Failure to pay your bills on time is one of the most detrimental actions you can take. Remember that late payments can drastically lower your credit score, making it more difficult to obtain credit in the future.

Additionally, be wary of predatory lending practices. Predatory lenders target individuals with poor credit, offering high-interest loans with unfavorable terms. Understand the specifics of a credit contract before agreeing to it and avoid any offer that looks too good to be true. If a contract is unclear or complex, seek a professional opinion from a trusted financial advisor. Don't feel pressured into signing anything you don't completely understand.

Effective credit management is a key component of long-term financial success. By understanding the basics of credit, building a positive credit history, and making informed decisions, you can leverage the power of credit to achieve your financial goals. However, remember that credit is a tool, and like any tool, it can be used for good or ill. Using it responsibly, carefully and cautiously, will allow it to become an asset rather than a liability. Develop a sound financial plan, incorporating budgeting techniques to help you avoid overspending and to track your financial progress.

In conclusion, utilizing credit wisely is a journey, not a destination. It requires consistent effort, responsible behavior, and a keen understanding of the credit system. By following the guidelines outlined above, you can build and maintain a strong credit history, enabling you to access favorable credit terms and achieve your long-term financial goals. The reward for disciplined credit management is not merely a high credit score, but enhanced financial freedom and security. Always remember that responsible credit management is a crucial element of achieving lasting financial success. Make it a priority and reap the considerable benefits.

Seeking Professional Financial Advice

Having established a solid understanding of credit management and its crucial role in building a robust financial foundation, it's time to discuss another vital component of achieving long-term financial security: seeking professional financial advice. While self-education and diligent personal management are essential, the complexities of modern finance often necessitate the expertise of a qualified professional. A financial advisor can provide personalized guidance, helping you navigate the intricacies of investing, debt management, and long-term financial planning, ultimately increasing the Likelihood of achieving your financial goals.

The benefits of working with a financial advisor are multifaceted. First and foremost, they bring a wealth of experience and knowledge to the table. They've witnessed market cycles, economic downturns, and periods of unprecedented growth, allowing them to offer insights based on years of practical experience. This experience translates to informed decision-making, helping you avoid costly mistakes that could significantly impact your financial Well-being. They can provide objective assessments of your financial situation, free from the emotional biases that can often cloud our judgment when making financial decisions.

A financial advisor can create a comprehensive financial plan tailored to your specific needs, goals, and risk tolerance. This plan acts as a roadmap, guiding your financial journey toward your desired destination – whether it's early retirement, funding your children's education, or ensuring a comfortable lifestyle in your later years. The plan will likely encompass a detailed analysis of your current financial situation, including assets, liabilities, income, and expenses. From there, the advisor will work with you to define your financial goals, both short-term and long-term. Based on this information, they will recommend strategies for achieving those goals, incorporating investment strategies, debt reduction plans, and risk management techniques.

The creation of a personalized financial plan is not a one-time event; it's an ongoing process that requires regular review and Adjustments. Your circumstances are likely to change over time – you may receive a promotion, get married, have children, or experience unexpected life events. A financial advisor can help you adapt your plan to these changes, ensuring it remains relevant and effective throughout your life. This regular review process is crucial for staying on track and making necessary corrections to keep your investments aligned with your goals and risk tolerance.

Furthermore, a financial advisor can provide invaluable assistance with investment management. Investing can be daunting, particularly for those unfamiliar with the complexities of the market. Financial advisors have the expertise to select suitable investments based on your risk tolerance, time horizon, and financial goals. They can diversify your portfolio to mitigate risk and help you navigate the ever-changing landscape of investment options. This is especially helpful in today's volatile economic climate. They can also manage your investments actively, adjusting your portfolio in response to market conditions to optimize returns.

Beyond investment management, financial advisors can offer expert guidance on debt management. They can help you develop a strategic plan for paying down debt, prioritizing high-interest debt and exploring options for debt consolidation or refinancing. Effective debt management is critical for long-term financial health, and a financial advisor can provide valuable support in this area. They can also assist in creating and maintaining a sound budget, which is often overlooked yet incredibly significant for sound financial management.

Finding a reputable financial advisor is just as crucial as understanding the benefits of seeking professional advice. Several factors should guide your search. First, consider their credentials and experience. Look for advisors who hold relevant professional certifications, such as a Certified Financial Planner (CFP) designation or a Chartered Financial Analyst (CFA) designation.

These certifications demonstrate a commitment to professional standards and ongoing education. Experience is also critical, as it provides invaluable insights and perspectives that enhance their ability to guide you effectively. Secondly, research their fee structure. Fees can vary significantly, so it's important to understand how the advisor is compensated. Some advisors charge a flat fee, while others charge a percentage of your assets under management. Clearly understand all costs associated with their services before engaging their help. Transparency in pricing is paramount, as hidden fees can quickly erode your investment returns.

Thirdly, check their background and reputation. Research the advisor's background to ensure they have a clean regulatory record, free from any disciplinary actions or complaints. Reviews and testimonials from past clients can provide additional insights into their work ethic and effectiveness. Be cautious of overly optimistic promises of quick riches or guaranteed returns. No reputable financial advisor would make such claims. If they do, consider it a significant red flag and immediately discontinue the relationship.

Finally, schedule a consultation to assess their suitability. A consultation allows you to discuss your financial goals, ask questions about their approach, and assess their suitability for your needs and personality. The relationship between you and your financial advisor is crucial, and it must be based on mutual trust, respect, and open communication. Ensure you feel comfortable with their demeanor and style. Remember, you are making a significant decision by entrusting someone with your financial well-being, and a great advisor will recognize this, fostering a mutually beneficial and respectful collaboration.

Seeking professional financial advice is not a luxury; it's an investment in your financial future. A qualified financial advisor can provide the guidance, support, and expertise needed to achieve your financial goals, helping you navigate the complexities of the financial world and build a secure financial future. It is a crucial step in the process of developing and maintaining a sustainable and successful financial plan. The insights, expertise, and support provided by a financial advisor can translate to a significant improvement in the success of your long-term financial strategy. Take the time to find a professional who aligns with your needs and goals, and embark on a journey towards greater financial success with confidence and clarity. Remember, you deserve to build a Stable and secure financial future, and utilizing the skills and experience of a competent advisor is a significant step toward accomplishing that goal.

Chapter 6: Staying Informed and Adapting To Economic Change

In today's rapidly evolving economic landscape, staying informed is not merely beneficial—it's essential for safeguarding your financial well-being. The information overload available through various media channels can be both a blessing and a curse. While access to data is unparalleled, discerning credible sources and interpreting the information accurately requires a discerning eye and a critical mindset. This section will equip you with the tools and knowledge to navigate this information landscape effectively, enabling you to make sound financial decisions amidst economic uncertainty.

One of the most powerful tools at your disposal is access to reliable financial news. Websites such as the *Wall Street Journal, Bloomberg, Financial Times,* and *Reuters* provide in-depth analyses, market updates, and economic commentary from seasoned professionals. These sources are generally reputable, adhering to journalistic standards and offering fact-checked information. However, even with reputable sources, it's crucial to approach the information with a critical eye, recognizing potential biases or conflicts of interest. For example, an article sponsored by a specific company might present a more positive view of that company's performance or outlook than an independent analysis would offer.

Beyond dedicated financial news outlets, reputable economic publications offer valuable insights into broader economic trends. Publications like *The Economist* provide comprehensive global economic analyses, covering macroeconomic indicators, geopolitical events, and their impact on various markets. These publications often employ teams of economists and analysts, providing well- researched and insightful articles. Remember to always cross- reference information; if a particular claim or prediction is found only in one obscure source, treat it with significant skepticism. A robust understanding of the subject matter requires considering diverse perspectives from multiple reliable sources.

Government reports and data releases offer invaluable insight into the state of the economy. Central banks, such as the Federal Reserve in the United States or the European Central Bank, regularly publish economic data, including inflation rates, interest rate decisions, and employment statistics. These reports provide a firsthand account of the economy's performance, allowing you to gain a deeper Understanding of the factors influencing market movements. These reports, however, often require a certain level of economic literacy to interpret fully. Don't be afraid to seek clarification from financial experts or educational resources if you find yourself struggling with the technical details.

Beyond official government publications, various independent research firms and think tanks also produce valuable economic analyses and forecasts. These organizations often conduct detailed research on specific sectors or industries, providing insights that may not be available through mainstream media sources. However, it's critical to evaluate the reputation and potential biases of these organizations. Look for organizations with a proven track record of objective analysis and transparency in their methodology. Be wary of organizations with overt political leanings, as their research might reflect those biases.

In addition to actively seeking information, you should develop a personalized system for filtering relevant information. This involves identifying the economic indicators and market trends that are most relevant to your investment portfolio and financial goals. For example, if you are heavily invested in the technology sector, you would benefit from closely monitoring technological advancements, regulatory changes, and consumer spending trends related to technology products and services. Similarly, if your investments are focused on real estate, tracking interest rates, housing starts, and employment rates is crucial. Tailoring your information intake to your specific investment strategy allows you to focus your attention on the most impactful data points, improving your decision-making efficiency.

One effective way to streamline the information gathering process is to subscribe to curated newsletters or podcasts that provide summaries of important economic news and trends. Many reputable financial institutions and analysts offer free or paid subscription services. These services often provide concise summaries of complex economic data, making them ideal for busy individuals who want to remain updated without dedicating extensive time to research. Be sure to carefully vet these services, just as you would any other source of information, and check for a history of accurate predictions or insightful analysis. However, the abundance of information also presents the significant challenge of misinformation. The internet is rife with unreliable information, ranging from misleading articles to outright scams. Developing critical thinking skills is paramount in navigating this landscape. When evaluating information, look for evidence of bias, conflicts of interest, or lack of supporting data. Cross-referencing information from multiple sources is crucial. If a claim is only found in one source or seems too good to be true, it warrants a high degree of skepticism. It is always wise to question the source's motivation and verify the information independently before making any significant financial decisions.

This emphasis on critical thinking extends to interpreting economic data. While economic indicators provide valuable insights, they do not offer guarantees. For instance, an increase in consumer spending doesn't necessarily equate to a booming economy; it could simply reflect increased inflation or debt-fueled purchases. A thorough understanding of economic principles and their interrelationships allows for a more nuanced interpretation of data. Understanding the limitations of economic models and projections is also critical to avoiding overly optimistic or pessimistic assessments.

Technological advancements have also significantly impacted the accessibility of economic information. Sophisticated data visualization tools allow you to analyze economic data in new and insightful ways. However, the potential for manipulating data or creating misleading visualizations is also present. Therefore, it is crucial to understand the underlying data and the methodology used to present it visually. Carefully examine charts and graphs for misleading scales or selective data presentations. Remember, a well-designed visualization should enhance understanding, not obscure the truth.

Developing a robust strategy for staying informed requires a multifaceted approach. Combine regular engagement with reputable financial news sources, careful analysis of government reports and economic publications, and the development of strong critical thinking skills. Regularly evaluate your sources, and continually adapt your approach as new information becomes available and as the information environment evolves. Remember, staying informed is an ongoing process that requires dedication and intellectual rigor. The effort is well worth it, however, as making informed decisions based on credible information greatly enhances the likelihood of achieving long-term financial success. The pursuit of financial knowledge should be a continuous journey, enriching your understanding of economic forces and positioning you to navigate market fluctuations with confidence.

Developing a Long-term Investment Strategy

Building a resilient investment portfolio requires more than just reacting to daily market headlines; it demands a well-defined, long- term strategy tailored to your individual circumstances. This strategy should be a roadmap, guiding your investment decisions through economic booms and busts, ensuring you stay focused on your ultimate financial goals. Remember, investing is a marathon, not a sprint. Short-term market fluctuations are inevitable, and attempting to time the market—trying to buy low and sell high based on short-term predictions—is often a losing game. The most successful investors are those who remain disciplined, patient, and focused on their long-term objectives.

The foundation of any robust long-term investment strategy lies in understanding your own financial goals and risk tolerance. What are you saving for? Retirement? A down payment on a house? Your child's education? Defining your goals provides a clear target, enabling you to select investment vehicles and strategies aligned with your timeline and risk appetite. If you're investing for Retirement decades away, you generally have more time to ride out market downturns and can afford to take on a higher level of risk. Conversely, if your investment goal is just a few years away, a more conservative approach, focused on preserving capital, is generally recommended.

Assessing your risk tolerance is equally critical. How comfortable are you with the possibility of short-term losses in exchange for the potential for higher long-term returns? Are you a conservative investor who prioritizes capital preservation above all else, or are you more aggressive, willing to accept greater risk for potentially higher gains? Honest self-assessment in this area is crucial in determining the appropriate asset allocation for your portfolio. This assessment shouldn't be a one-time event; as your life circumstances change, so too should your risk tolerance and investment strategy.

Once you've defined your financial goals and risk tolerance, you can begin constructing your portfolio. Diversification is key. Don't put all your eggs in one basket. Spread your investments across Different asset classes, such as stocks, bonds, real estate, and potentially alternative investments like commodities or precious metals. The specific allocation will depend on your individual risk tolerance and time horizon. A younger investor with a longer time horizon might allocate a larger portion of their portfolio to stocks, which historically have offered higher returns than bonds, even with increased volatility. An older investor closer to retirement, on the other hand, might favor a more conservative allocation with a larger percentage in bonds to protect their principal.

We've previously explored various investment options, including certificates of deposit (CDs), annuities, higher-yield savings accounts, and different stock classifications (aggressive growth, medium-aggressive, and safe, low-risk). Remember the importance of understanding the risk-reward profile of each investment. Higher potential returns generally come with higher risk. The key lies in finding the right balance for your personal circumstances. Consider exploring index funds or exchange-traded funds (ETFs) for broad market exposure and diversification. These funds allow you to invest in a basket of securities, offering instant diversification without the need for extensive individual stock picking.

Emerging markets, like those in the AI and electronics/chip manufacturing sectors, offer exciting potential but also carry significant risk. Investing in these sectors requires careful due diligence and a thorough understanding of the underlying technologies and market dynamics. Remember to research the companies you're considering thoroughly, examining their financial statements, competitive landscape, and management team. Don't rely solely on hype or short-term price movements.

Precious metals like gold and silver are often considered a safe haven asset, offering a hedge against inflation and economic uncertainty. However, they typically offer lower returns compared to other asset classes and should only make up a small portion of a well-diversified portfolio. Their value fluctuates based on various factors, including global economic conditions and investor sentiment. Understanding these dynamics is crucial before including them in your investment strategy.

Regularly reviewing and rebalancing your portfolio is another critical component of a long-term strategy. Market conditions change, and your individual circumstances may evolve over time. Therefore, periodic portfolio reviews are necessary to ensure it remains aligned with your goals and risk tolerance. Rebalancing involves adjusting your portfolio's asset allocation to bring it back to your target allocation. This process may involve selling some assets that have appreciated beyond their target allocation and buying others that have underperformed. Rebalancing helps to prevent excessive risk concentration in any single asset class.

Patience and discipline are paramount in long-term investing. Avoid the temptation to make impulsive decisions based on short-term market movements or emotional reactions. Stay focused on your long-term goals and stick to your investment plan, even during periods of market volatility. This consistency is crucial for long-term success. Remember that market downturns are an inevitable part of the investment cycle. They can be unsettling, but they also present opportunities to buy high-quality assets at discounted prices. Disciplined investors who remain calm and focused during these periods are often rewarded in the long run.

A crucial element frequently overlooked is the importance of ongoing education. The economic landscape is continuously changing, influenced by technological advancements, geopolitical events, and evolving regulatory frameworks. Remaining updated on economic trends and investment strategies is essential to make informed decisions and adapt your portfolio as necessary. This doesn't require you to become a financial expert, but continuous learning, whether through reading reputable financial publications, attending seminars, or consulting with a financial advisor, will significantly enhance your investment knowledge and decision- making abilities.

Your long-term investment strategy should also consider inflation. Inflation erodes the purchasing power of your savings over time. Therefore, your investments need to generate returns that outpace inflation to maintain your financial well-being. Understanding inflation's impact on your investments is crucial in selecting appropriate investment vehicles and adjusting your portfolio's asset Allocation.

Tax implications are another important factor. Different investment vehicles have different tax implications. Understanding these implications can significantly impact your overall investment returns. For example, some investments offer tax advantages, such as tax- deferred growth or tax-free distributions. Consulting with a tax professional can help you optimize your investment strategy to minimize your tax burden.

Finally, consider seeking guidance from a qualified financial advisor. A financial advisor can provide personalized advice tailored to your specific financial goals, risk tolerance, and Circumstances. They can help you create a comprehensive financial plan, select appropriate investment vehicles, and monitor your portfolio's performance. While a financial advisor's services may come with a fee, their expertise and objective perspective can be invaluable in navigating the complexities of long-term investing.

In conclusion, developing a successful long-term investment strategy is a multifaceted process that requires careful planning, discipline, and ongoing education. By understanding your financial goals, assessing your risk tolerance, diversifying your investments, regularly reviewing and rebalancing your portfolio, and staying informed about economic trends, you can significantly increase your chances of achieving long-term financial success. Remember that investing is a journey, not a destination. Stay focused on your goals, remain patient and disciplined, and adapt your strategy as needed to navigate the ever-changing economic landscape.

Adapting Your Portfolio to Economic Shifts

Adapting your investment portfolio to economic shifts is not merely reactive; it's a proactive strategy that requires continuous monitoring and adjustments. Economic landscapes are dynamic, influenced by a complex interplay of factors ranging from geopolitical instability and technological disruption to shifts in consumer confidence and government policies. Ignoring these changes can significantly impact your portfolio's performance and your long-term financial goals.

One of the most significant economic indicators to track is inflation. Inflation, the rate at which prices for goods and services increase, directly impacts the purchasing power of your money. High inflation erodes the value of your investments, meaning that your returns might not keep pace with the rising cost of living. During inflationary periods, it's crucial to re-evaluate your portfolio's asset allocation. Traditional safe haven assets like bonds might underperform, as their fixed income struggles to outpace rising prices. Consider shifting a greater portion of your portfolio towards Assets that historically provide inflation hedges, such as real estate, commodities (particularly gold and other precious metals), and equities of companies with strong pricing power – those capable of passing increased costs onto consumers. Inflation-linked bonds, or TIPS (Treasury Inflation-Protected Securities), are specifically designed to protect against inflation; their principal adjusts with the Consumer Price Index (CPI), helping maintain purchasing power.

Recessions, periods of significant economic decline, present another significant challenge for investors. During recessions, unemployment rises, consumer spending decreases, and business profits often fall. These conditions typically lead to lower stock market valuations and increased volatility. A well-diversified portfolio can help mitigate some of the risks associated with recessions. However, even with diversification, you may need to adjust your strategy. Consider shifting towards more defensive investments like high-quality bonds, dividend-paying stocks with robust balance sheets, and cash equivalents. These assets tend to be less susceptible to the sharp downturns characteristic of recessions.

It's crucial to resist panic selling during a recession. Market downturns, though unsettling, often present buying opportunities for long-term investors. Disciplined investors can acquire high-quality assets at discounted prices, setting themselves up for greater potential gains when the economy recovers. Remember, history has shown that economic downturns are temporary.

Interest rate changes, implemented by central banks to control inflation and economic growth, also significantly impact investment portfolios. Interest rate hikes typically lead to higher borrowing costs for businesses and consumers, which can slow economic activity. This often negatively affects growth stocks, which are valued based on future earnings expectations. Conversely, interest rate cuts can stimulate economic growth, leading to a rise in stock prices. When interest rates rise, consider shifting from growth stocks to value stocks, companies with lower valuations relative to their earnings and assets. Value stocks tend to be less sensitive to interest rate changes. Furthermore, rising interest rates often benefit fixed- income securities like bonds, as their yields become more attractive. Conversely, when interest rates fall, growth stocks might become more attractive, as investors are willing to pay a premium for companies with high future growth potential.

Another critical aspect of adapting your portfolio is risk management. This involves actively identifying and mitigating potential risks to your investments. Risk management techniques range from diversification (spreading investments across different asset classes) to hedging (using financial instruments to offset potential losses) and stop-loss orders (pre-set instructions to sell an asset if it falls below a certain price). Employing various risk management techniques enables you to protect your capital during periods of market volatility and maintain your overall investment strategy.

The 2008 financial crisis offers a compelling illustration of how economic events can impact portfolios. Investors heavily invested in subprime mortgages experienced substantial losses, while those with diversified portfolios and a focus on defensive assets fared better. Similarly, the

COVID-19 pandemic induced a sharp market downturn, impacting various sectors differently. Companies in the Travel and hospitality industries suffered, while those involved in technology and essential goods thrived. Adapting portfolio allocations based on industry-specific vulnerabilities and growth opportunities during these periods is crucial for optimizing returns.

The tech bubble burst of the early 2000s also serves as a cautionary tale. Investors who heavily concentrated their holdings in Technology stocks experienced significant losses. This highlights the importance of diversification and avoiding excessive concentration in any single sector. Always maintain a balanced portfolio aligned with your risk tolerance, considering various economic conditions.

Successfully navigating economic shifts requires flexibility and adaptability. No single investment strategy works perfectly under all conditions. Regularly reviewing your portfolio's performance and adjusting its composition in response to changing economic conditions is essential. This process is not solely about reacting to market movements; it's also about proactively identifying potential risks and opportunities, based on your ongoing economic and market research. Staying informed about relevant economic indicators, geopolitical events, and industry trends is a critical component of this process.

This involves more than just following daily market news. You need to understand the underlying economic principles driving market movements. Understanding economic cycles, inflation dynamics, and monetary policy decisions is vital for making informed investment choices. Consider subscribing to reputable financial publications, attending seminars, or consulting with a financial advisor. These resources can provide valuable insights and guidance in navigating complex economic conditions and adapting your portfolio.

Furthermore, regularly rebalancing your portfolio is crucial to maintain your target asset allocation. Rebalancing involves selling assets that have appreciated beyond their target allocation and buying assets that have underperformed. This helps to control risk by preventing overexposure to any single asset class and ensuring your portfolio aligns with your risk tolerance and investment goals.

In conclusion, successfully adapting your investment portfolio to economic shifts demands a proactive, data-driven approach. By closely monitoring key economic indicators, understanding the impact of various economic events, and proactively managing risk, you can build a more resilient portfolio capable of weathering economic uncertainty and achieving long-term financial success.

Remember, flexibility, adaptability, and continuous learning are vital components in navigating the complexities of the ever-Changing economic landscape. The ability to adjust your strategy in response to economic conditions will ultimately determine your success in the long run. Continuous education and a willingness to adapt are your greatest allies in this process.

The Importance of Continuous Learning in Investing

The ability to adapt and adjust your investment strategy is paramount in today's dynamic economic climate. However, adaptability is not a passive trait; it's a skill honed through continuous learning and a commitment to staying abreast of the ever-evolving financial landscape. The markets are constantly shifting, influenced by a myriad of factors, from technological breakthroughs and geopolitical events to changes in consumer behavior and regulatory environments. Relying on outdated knowledge or a static investment approach is a recipe for underperformance, potentially jeopardizing your long-term financial goals.

Continuous learning in investing isn't just about staying informed; it's about cultivating a mindset of intellectual curiosity and a Proactive approach to acquiring new knowledge. This process involves far more than passively consuming daily market news reports. True mastery requires a deep understanding of fundamental economic principles, market mechanics, and the psychology driving investor behavior. It means delving into the underlying forces shaping market trends and making informed decisions based on sound analytical reasoning rather than reacting emotionally to short- term fluctuations.

One effective method for continuous learning is to actively seek out reputable sources of financial information. This might involve subscribing to respected financial publications, both print and digital, that offer in-depth analysis and expert commentary. Look for publications that go beyond simply reporting market movements and delve into the underlying economic factors driving those movements. Publications that provide rigorous analysis and diverse perspectives will be more beneficial than those that offer simplistic, sensationalized coverage.

Beyond formal publications, attending workshops and seminars can significantly enhance your knowledge base. These events often feature presentations by experienced financial professionals, offering valuable insights and practical strategies that might not be readily available in print or online. Look for workshops that cover a range of topics, including portfolio diversification, risk management, and specific investment strategies. The networking Opportunities at such events also offer invaluable access to insights and perspectives from your peers.

The internet, while a source of a great deal of unreliable information, can also be a powerful tool for continuous learning. However, it is crucial to critically evaluate the sources you consult online. Look for websites and blogs maintained by reputable financial institutions, academic researchers, or experienced investment professionals. Be wary of websites or social media influencers promoting get-rich-quick schemes or providing unsubstantiated investment advice. Always verify information found online with multiple reliable sources before making any investment decisions.

Continuous learning also involves developing strong analytical skills. This includes the ability to critically evaluate financial statements, understand market trends, and interpret economic data. Learning how to interpret complex financial reports, such as balance sheets and income statements, is crucial for evaluating the financial health and potential of individual companies. Understanding macroeconomic indicators, such as inflation, unemployment rates, and interest rates, provides context for assessing overall market conditions and their potential impact on your investments.

Furthermore, understanding behavioral finance is another critical aspect of continuous learning. Behavioral finance recognizes the influence of psychological factors on investment decisions. Understanding cognitive biases, such as overconfidence and herd mentality, can help you avoid making emotional decisions that might harm your portfolio. Learning to recognize and mitigate these biases is a crucial skill for long-term investment success.

The development of strong analytical and critical-thinking skills often requires a dedicated effort. This might involve taking online courses, reading books on financial analysis, or even pursuing formal financial education. Many reputable universities and online Platforms offer courses in finance, investing, and economics. These courses can provide a structured approach to learning and offer the opportunity to earn professional certifications.

Staying informed is an ongoing process that should be woven into your daily or weekly routine. Make a commitment to dedicate time, even if it's just 30 minutes to an hour each week, to staying current with economic and market developments. Follow key economic indicators, read financial news, and review your investment portfolio's performance. This consistent effort will contribute significantly to your ability to adapt your investment strategy as needed.

Technological advancements are also rapidly changing the investment landscape. The rise of Fintech, algorithmic trading, and Robot-advisors has introduced new tools and platforms for investors. Staying informed about these technological changes and understanding how they might impact your investment strategies is becoming increasingly important. Exploring new technologies and platforms can help you streamline your investment process and potentially improve your returns. However, always exercise caution when using new technologies and ensure that the platforms you are using are secure and reputable.

Finally, remember that continuous learning is a lifelong pursuit. The investment world is constantly evolving, with new opportunities and challenges emerging regularly. Embracing this continuous learning process is not just about accumulating knowledge; it's about cultivating a growth mindset – a willingness to adapt, learn from mistakes, and evolve your investment approach to meet the changing realities of the market. This ongoing commitment to education and self-improvement is the key to navigating the complexities of investing and achieving your long-term financial goals. The investor who stands still risks falling behind; the investor who continuously learns remains adaptable, resilient, and poised for success. In a volatile economy, continuous learning is not just an advantage; it is a necessity for long-term success. It is the foundation upon which sound, adaptable investment strategies are built.

Building a Sustainable Financial Future

Building a sustainable financial future requires a holistic approach that extends beyond simply choosing the right investments. It's about creating a robust financial plan that aligns with your personal goals, risk tolerance, and long-term aspirations. This plan should encompass not only investment strategies but also budgeting, debt management, and estate planning. A well-structured financial plan acts as a roadmap, guiding you toward financial security and independence.

One of the cornerstones of a sustainable financial future is consistent saving and investing. The power of compounding returns over time is undeniable. The earlier you begin saving and investing, the greater the potential for growth, thanks to the snowball effect of earning returns on your returns. Even small, regular contributions to a retirement account or investment portfolio can accumulate significantly over decades. Consistency is key; don't let market fluctuations derail you're long-term saving and investment plan. Instead, view them as opportunities to adjust your strategy, potentially buying low when assets are temporarily depressed.

Diversification plays a crucial role in mitigating risk and building a resilient portfolio. Don't put all your eggs in one basket. Spread your investments across different asset classes, such as stocks, bonds, real estate, and alternative assets like gold or commodities. This diversification helps to reduce the impact of any single investment underperforming. Within each asset class, you can further diversify your holdings by investing in different sectors, companies, and geographies. The ideal diversification strategy depends on your individual risk tolerance and financial goals. For example, a younger investor with a longer time horizon may tolerate more risk and allocate a larger portion of their portfolio to equities, while an older investor nearing retirement might prefer a more conservative approach with a greater emphasis on fixed-income investments.

Regularly reviewing and rebalancing your portfolio is essential to maintain your desired asset allocation. Over time, the value of your Investments will fluctuate, causing your asset allocation to drift from your target. Rebalancing involves selling some of your higher- performing assets and buying more of your underperforming assets to restore your desired allocation. This strategy helps to lock in profits from your winners while taking advantage of potential buying opportunities in your underperforming assets. The frequency of rebalancing depends on your individual circumstances and investment strategy. Some investors rebalance annually, while others do so quarterly or even semiannually.

Debt management is another crucial aspect of building a sustainable financial future. High levels of debt can significantly hinder your ability to save and invest. Prioritize paying down high-interest debt, such as credit card debt, before focusing on lower-interest debt, like student loans or mortgages. Develop a realistic budget to track your income and expenses, identifying areas where you can reduce spending and allocate more resources toward debt repayment and saving. Consider exploring debt consolidation strategies to simplify your payments and potentially lower your interest rates.

Estate planning is often overlooked but is an essential component of long-term financial security. It involves creating a plan for the distribution of your assets after your death. This planning minimizes potential family disputes and ensures your assets are distributed according to your wishes. Key elements of estate planning include drafting a will, establishing a trust, and designating beneficiaries for your retirement accounts and other assets. Consult with an estate planning attorney to develop a comprehensive plan that aligns with your specific needs and circumstances.

The role of professional guidance cannot be overstated in building a sustainable financial future. While self-directed investing is possible, seeking advice from a qualified financial advisor can provide invaluable support and guidance. A financial advisor can help you develop a personalized financial plan, manage your investments, and navigate complex financial decisions. They can provide objective insights, unbiased advice, and a framework for making informed choices. Remember to choose a fiduciary advisor, one legally bound to act in your best interest. Finally, continuous learning is paramount in adapting to the ever- changing economic landscape. The financial world is dynamic; what worked yesterday might not work tomorrow. Stay informed about economic trends, investment strategies, and relevant legislation by reading financial publications, attending seminars, and utilizing reputable online resources. Remember to critically evaluate the information you consume, focusing on reliable sources and expert opinions. Continuous learning empowers you to adjust your strategy as needed, ensuring your financial plan remains relevant and effective in the face of unforeseen challenges.

In conclusion, building a sustainable financial future is a multifaceted journey requiring proactive planning, consistent effort, and a commitment to lifelong learning. By combining prudent saving and investing habits, effective debt management, Comprehensive estate planning, and ongoing professional guidance, you can create a robust and resilient financial foundation to secure your future and achieve your financial aspirations. Remember, while the market may fluctuate, your commitment to a well-defined financial plan will provide the stability and direction necessary to navigate economic uncertainty and achieve long-term success. This requires discipline, patience, and a willingness to adapt your strategies as needed. The journey is long, but the rewards of a secure financial future are well worth the effort. The knowledge gained throughout this book equips you with the essential tools and strategies to embark on this rewarding journey. Now, it's up to you to take the next step and start building your sustainable financial future.

Acknowledgments

Thank You

I am deeply grateful to the many individuals who played a part in bringing this book to life. Expressing my heartfelt gratitude, I begin with my wife, and her unwavering support and belief in my creative pursuit were the foundation upon which this book was built. She provided the encouragement I needed to embark on this journey, and her presence continued to inspire me throughout the process. Her role in this endeavor was integral, and I am forever thankful for the ways in which she challenged and motivated me.

Her influence extended beyond the realm of emotional support; her insights and feedback on the content of this book were invaluable. Through her thoughtful critiques and encouraging words, she helped shape and refine my work. As I reflect on the completion of this book, I am overwhelmed by a sense of gratitude for the people in my life who made it possible.

My wife, with her unwavering support and insightful contributions, holds a special place in my heart. This accomplishment is a testament to the power of collaboration and the enduring impact of those who believe in us and their unwavering support and patience throughout the writing process. Their understanding and encouragement were invaluable. Finally, I thank all those who provided feedback and encouragement along the way – your contributions were instrumental in shaping the final product.

Appendix

This appendix provides supplementary information to enhance the reader's understanding of the concepts discussed in the book. It includes:

Appendix A: Glossary of Financial Terms:

A more comprehensive glossary of terms than the one in the main body of the book. (Note: This information is also included in the Glossary section below.)

Glossary

Glossary of Financial Terms:

401(k): A retirement savings plan sponsored by employers.

Annuities: Financial products providing a stream of payments over time.

Asset Allocation: The distribution of investments across various asset classes.

Bear Market: A prolonged period of declining stock prices.

Bonds: Debt securities issued by governments or corporations. **Bull Market:** A prolonged period of rising stock prices.

CD (Certificate of Deposit): A savings account with a fixed interest rate and term.

Diversification: Spreading investments across different asset classes to reduce risk.

Emerging Markets: Economies with rapid growth potential.

Equities: Stocks representing ownership in a company.

Fixed-Income Investments: Investments with predictable returns.
Mutual Funds: Investments pooling money from multiple investors.
Portfolio: A collection of investments.

Risk Tolerance: An investor's capacity to accept potential losses.

Stocks: Shares of ownership in a company.

References

The contents and information of this book represents years of knowledge gained from research and from numerous friends, family, and personal financial advisers.

Author Biography

The Author, Steve Dean, hopes that reading his book will help everyone in making wiser decisions with their investments so their retirement 401K's; or whatever type of investments they pursue, will grow nicely for them. The research done in making this book was to help get a better understanding of financial planning and then to pass this on to help others do the same. Hopefully, this will empower others to make better informed decisions and feel more confident about their savings.

Here's to you and your financial success!